This paperback edition published by Canongate Books in 2022

First published in Great Britain in 2021 by Canongate Books Ltd,
14 High Street, Edinburgh EH1 1TE

canongate.co.uk

1

*British Library Cataloguing-in-Publication Data*
A catalogue record for this book is available on
request from the British Library

ISBN 978 1 78689 964 4

Typeset in Bembo by Palimpsest Book Production Ltd,
Falkirk, Stirlingshire

Printed and bound in Great Britain by Clays Ltd, Elcograf S.p.A.

MIX
Paper from
responsible sources
FSC
www.fsc.org    FSC® C018072

# THIN PLACES

### KERRI NÍ DOCHARTAIGH

CANONGATE

*for the people,*
*for the places,*
*for those lost,*
*for those moths.*

# Contents

PART TWO: FEATHER AND STONE

# Prologue

WHEN I FIRST SEE HER she is as still as a found stone, in an ancient and hidden place. She stands out, a quiet caller of the eye – her markings blend in so delicately in this place, against the grasses and the thistle, the sand that marks the Atlantic Ocean from the land. I am at *An tSrúibh* – Shroove Beach – completely alone, miles across the border from my home in Derry, when we cross one another's path.

She looks so calm, unstirring in spite of the winds that now set the tall grasses on the beach to dance. She is so beautiful – I may even call her celestial – that I almost feel I have no right to be here. In this moment, in this place, with this graceful wonder, what part can I play in her story, in the narrative of this ethereal offering of a creature? I begin to feel that I am not, in fact, even 'seeing' her. It is more an act of witness. There is so little action in the small part I play on this near-winter morning, at a part of the Inishowen Peninsula where Lough Foyle meets the wild Atlantic, at the edge-land of Donegal, in one of the most northerly places on the island of Ireland.

We have found ourselves in a state of turmoil here, in the North of Ireland, and all the other parts that make up the United Kingdom are caught up in the same storm. It is November 2019, and next month the first Christmas Election in decades will take place. The air has been charged for many months with worry and confusion but none of that seems real, here, amidst such silent serenity.

She dances. She is the centre of it all, the still point on the map, a heavenly and delicate thing, too sacred for words. I am only the beholder, here, and I am drinking it all in. I bathe in her silent, gossamer grace. I watch her for what feels like a hundred years – one hundred years and this one, solitary day. The winter sun is high enough above the lighthouse to make the reeds double on themselves. Their silhouettes now join her in shadow play; they seem as if they are weaving themselves together and dancing in time with her. I am on my own, on the outside, looking in at the reeds and the moth; as if I am on the other side of an ice-sculpted lake or a mirror. They are right here beside me yet they feel so completely out of reach.

I tiptoe around the edges, and I feel myself outside time, as well as place. Now I am in both and in neither all at once.

I gratefully wait on the threshold, holding my breath as the reeds dance, grass goddesses on the hushed dunes, beside an ethereal, exquisite *leamhan*.

A winter moth, in a weightless, willowy place.

I begin to dry myself. The water today was icy and the sea's waves tall and white as snow, like mountains she had given birth to overnight. I am shivering, now, violently, on the wet

November sand, but I feel like I have been made new, somehow. There is almost full silence. All that undoes it are the soft sounds of the *dreoilín* – a wren – and the water as it ebbs and flows out at the horizon.

Then, all out of nowhere a deep, melancholy cry rings out over the dunes. A call that speaks of wildness, of solitude, of survival and unimaginable beauty. Twelve curlews are in flight in the sky above my head, calling out over the edges of the eastern coast of the Inishowen Peninsula. They are the same colour as the dunes, the grasses and the other winged creature on the beach, that almost otherworldly moth. Their call is haunting – a siren song written long ago, and it drags me with it: out of myself, and back in again – out and in, like a wing-beat, or ebbing breath.

They have long held a place in our history as a marker, these folkloric birds: of the past, of the cruel and melancholy passing of time with all its irrevocable changes. The curlew's cry has shape-shifted into mournful lament – an elegy for all that is lost. For centuries, it has been taken as a sign of unbidden sorrow yet to come; the cries of those whistlers is a sound steeped in foreboding. Those creatures of coast, marsh and bog carrying disaster and grief, carefully, in the fine curves of their bills. This beach on which I stand, shivering and silvered by the salt of the Atlantic Ocean, is a perfect place for them – open, empty and desolate, at first glance. This beach – Shroove, Stroove, or Strove, depending on where you grew up – has a quality to it, a stillness, which lets me almost float away. It allows me to see things differently. It is as if the veil between worlds has become as thin as moth-wing. The lines that are normally drawn for and by us – between here and there, between now and then – seem as though they have been washed away, on some days. I shiver again, pull my arms in around the curve of my body and wonder if it is the sea that has made ghosts of what we think we know here, in this wee nook at this most northerly tip on this divided, broken island.

This shipping lane has been used for hundreds of years by ships carrying Irish emigrants to land far from where I stand – England, America, Australia, Canada. This rugged coastline has not only transported people, it has *stolen* them, too. She is a hungry sea, this one I am drawn to – pulled towards, tidally. She has claimed hundreds of ships, taken innumerable lives; the body of water in front of me holds a story of deepest loss within her belly.

Now, through the lifting mist, Ballycastle – in the north of Ireland – comes into view, only just. One moment the coastline is there, and then it isn't. It is a fleeting and flighty thing today, the outline of that other place across the sea – and border – from me. There are times at which, under certain conditions, Scotland can be seen from where I am standing, as clearly as if it were right there in front of you, as if you could hold it tenderly inside your own salty, shaky hands. Today is not one of those days. The only land that I can see from here is still in Ireland, across an invisible border, parts of both its sides are held in place by the ancient, changeable and wild Atlantic in front of me. This border – unseen, hand-drawn by man, and *for* him alone, too – has been the thread that has run through my life. A ghost vein on the map of my insides, it is a line that is political, physical, economical and geographical; yet it is a line I have never once set eyes upon. This invisible line – a border that skims the water I have just emerged from, as though it were a dragonfly – has been the cause of such sorrow and suffering, such trauma and loss, that I ran from its curves and coursing flow at the very first chance I got.

I was half the age I am now when I left my hometown. The year that I moved back, the UK voted to leave the EU. Despite the words about unity, solidarity and strength in togetherness, lots of people decided they wanted to choose a different path. Derry – my border town in the north-west of Ireland – known for being the place 'the Troubles' began, voted to remain. There is a very particular type of wisdom that is born out of witnessing unimaginable cruelty, out of the experience of dark, harrowing sorrow. I remember standing on this same beach just after that vote and weeping, memories surging through my insides like hidden tributaries. No more, no more, no more – we have all had enough already, enough for many lifetimes. That border has become a thread in the lives of so many more people between that day in 2016 and this one, three and a half years later.

The fog has lifted a little; to the right of me, its silky grey veil is still laid too low to allow the outline of Scotland to come into view. Now, just below the lighthouse, the *crotach* – the curlews – grace the middle part of the sky again. They are heading round the curve of the bay towards Greencastle, maybe even onwards yet. Maybe they are flying away from here, where

Lough Foyle floods into the Atlantic Ocean, to follow the flow of the river across the border and into the North. Or maybe they will turn the other way, chart a path over fossil-traced bog-land, above gorse and *ceannbhán* – bog-cotton – where butterflies and moths have left fragments of their tissue wings. Maybe today they will choose to fly above estuary and stream, over the mountains of the Donegal Gaeltacht, their cries blending together with words in the native tongue of those they fly above, in the South. They nest all over this land, those of them that are left, on both sides of the border.

The season is turning; I felt it so fully in the water today. November's full moon marks the birth of a new Celtic year, at the same time as symbolising an end, the death of the old year. It is known as the mourning moon in Pagan tradition. In many cultures, this full moon is intimately connected with death and loss, on both a literal and symbolic level. Some folk call it the snow or fog moon, and I can both feel and see why, today, as I shiver beneath sea fog that hides the sun away. There is a pale yellow-grey hue to it, and a softness that could easily bring the snow. My ancestors knew it as the reed moon. I watch as the *giolcach* – the reeds – move about in the icy breeze, and I imagine my ancestors watching too, from a place, like the full moon, that I cannot see.

To the Druids and the Celts, almost everything in the natural world was tied in some way to the greater being – the spirit – of the earth. For our ancestors, our role in it all as guardians was one of unshakeable magnitude. In Ogham – ancient writing on stone – the letters are named for trees, an alphabet of arboreal forms, only some of which are still known to us. The etymology of the word 'ogham' is not fully known but it may have roots in the Irish *og úaim* – 'point-seam' – the trace left over by the point of a sharp weapon, the midway mark. The stones on which the writings are carved are themselves a form of marker, too. And the places in which they are found are sometimes as thin as a reed.

The reeds are ready for cutting now, in November; their strong roots will still bind the soil along the banks together the whole year through, a delicate winter weaving. In ancient times, reeds were held as guardians. They are the botanical marker for the days around Samhain – when, it was believed, the veil between worlds lifts – until 24 November: the date, almost a year ago, when I decided to stop drinking. I had no idea about the significance of the date until now. The reed's power, in Celtic tradition, is protection.

This *gealach*, this moon, the one I cannot see but that I know is there, is the last one before the winter solstice, and it is the last one I will stand beneath in this place; for how long, I am unsure. By the time the velvet darkness of the solstice has covered the winter land, I will already be far from these reeds and the moth, the lighthouse and the curlews. I will be far from Shroove, from Donegal, from Derry; I will be too far from here to be seen, no matter what the light is doing above the sea.

No more, enough already: the moment is here to leave. I have carried too much sorrow into this water for one lifetime. The tide is shifting; the moment in Derry – in the North –

across the UK in general – is uncertain, and full of that same hidden violence I spent my childhood stepping over like delicate eggshells, just waiting for it to erupt. I cannot, and will not, live through it all again. I am making ready to leave the city in which I was born; I am leaving its feathery ghosts here – where its river meets the sea.

Enough already: this time I am able, and ready, to leave. The time spent here has changed everything, unravelled all the threads that had long been tangled up in messy, rotting knots; nothing feels how it did before, and for that I am fiercely grateful.

There are places – like this one – which are so thin that you meet yourself in the still point. Like the lifting of the silky veil on Samhain, you are held in the space in between. No matter the past, the present or what is yet to come. There is nothing you can do but listen for the gap in the silence, the change in the wind.

The right moment, when it comes, calls you up, up; calls you into a wind that lifts you. A wind that carries you with it, on its tails.

Watch.

First the curlews, next the moth, and now – you.

# PART ONE

## *Blood and Bone*

# CHAPTER ONE

## *Leamhain Bhána* – White Moths

You are standing on the banks of a river that you may have never seen before – that you may, in fact, never see. This river courses along a line that cuts the land up like a body; this river is a border invisible to the living.

The land is as still as it was in the very beginning, back when the ice melted away, and the light that it holds is folding itself into everything around you. Into the edges of the grey-blue water, into the ancient, lichen-covered rocks, into the gaps in between things, into you as you stand inside the vast, bright silence.

It is the winter solstice. The year is getting itself ready to turn; the land that you are held by is holding its breath. You and that land are making ready to wait. Snow, not yet here, is on the wind, hidden in a part of the sky you cannot see. All at once, from no place at all – softly and without any sign – comes the cinematic beating of wings, powerful and haunting. The salmon-pink December sky above, for the most fleeting of moments, is a world all of its own, a place unlike any you have ever known before.

You are standing on the banks of a river that has witnessed things that neither you nor I could ever begin to name.

You are standing on the banks of the River Foyle – at a place where north is south and where south is north – as a perfect V of whooper swans calls you home, back to that thin place in between.

•

Time, as we know it, is the original shape-shifter. Now the line of it runs straight as an old railway track; now it is a circle – many circles, in fact. Now it dances without moving – to and fro across millennia – around the whole turning world, filling the night sky with bounding green lights. Past, future, present: the unbidden, ineffable gift of it all. Memory is like a white moth in flight. Sometimes she comes so close that we can see the light falling into the hidden parts of ancient markings. On other days we cannot see her but we feel the delicate wing-beat down deep, in beside our bones.

The story, our own, is a shared one, of the lines and circles of the land we know, of the sorrow it has known and of our own white moth of memory.

Moths have been flying in the skies of this earth for millions of what we call years; some may even have been around for 190 million of these markers of passing eras, these dividers of time we have created by which to record and to remember.

The lands and the seas above which they have journeyed have changed vastly in this time; they are changing still. The land I know best, Ériu, Éire, Ireland – 'the goddess' – was often completely covered in a cloak of ice. The ice melted back then, as it continues to melt today. Now there is no part of the interior of Ireland that is further than seventy miles from the sea. This goddess-island is bounded by a two-thousand-mile coastline, one of ever-changing moods, fringed by rocky coves and beaches, dotted with clusters of islands of various sizes, more than one island for every day of the year. The outline of Ireland has been buffeted since its earliest days by the wild Atlantic Ocean, creating a seaboard of unrivalled beauty. The sea, the winds and the ice of millennia have worked together to sculpt a landscape that is as raw as it is gentle, full of nuance.

The earliest record of human presence on this island is from 12,500 years ago. In the fifth century CE, the island was Christianised, and by the twelfth century – following a Norman invasion – a neighbouring body of land, England, had claimed sovereignty. Two centuries and two decades ago, in 1801, the island became part of the United Kingdom through the Acts of Union. In the century that followed, the land and sea saw a War of Independence, which ended with the partition of the island. In May of 1921, just as the bluebells would have been filling the land with colour, Ireland was cut up into two parts – the 'Irish Free State' in the south of the island, and Northern Ireland, which remained a part of the United Kingdom, linked to the larger island across the water. The Irish border, that invisible line that cuts this island in two, has been around for a single century. A small speck of dust from the wing of a moth, a wee gap in a fossil found on a beach, that line that has defined the lives – and resulted in the deaths – of so many people has been around for the whole of my lifetime. Europe is defined, in many ways, by borders. They speak of crumbled empires, shifting boundaries – most of them, certainly the Irish border, speak of unimaginable suffering.

Eon, era, period, epoch: we are a race that has long sought to break things up, to divide, to separate, to draw lines between things that might otherwise have remained as one. My grandfather, one of the most important people in my life, was born less than a handful of days before this island was divided in two. The year I was born, Madonna's song 'Borderline' reached number one in Ireland. My island was the only place in the whole wide world where this song gained such acclaim. Madonna's 'borderline' was a made-up boundary which her love kept being pushed over. My borderline runs for 310 miles, cutting through walls, farms, lakes, rivers, roads, villages and bridges. My borderline is geographical in that it roughly follows water courses, in accordance with remnants of seventeenth-century county limits. My borderline is, in reality, a political line no one can fully understand, no matter how strongly the charcoal strokes have been laid on the page.

•

I am in my first year at primary school in my divided, broken city of Derry. I am living in the Waterside – the mostly Protestant side of town – in a rough, sectarian council estate. My parents are in their very early twenties. I had come along when they were teenagers. They were unmarried and had known each other less than a year when I was whispered of. Something they *did* know of one another – in spite of this shared future they now had in common – was their vastly different pasts. My mother is Catholic, my father Protestant. In the early 1980s in the city of Doire-Derry-Londonderry, at the height of the period of unthinkable violence known as 'the Troubles' such a pairing was exceptionally rare. Division between the two sides – Protestant and Catholic – was very much the norm. Folk from either side of the River Foyle – a natural boundary which easily marked out where your individual background allowed you to safely walk – went to school separately, to church, to sports events, funerals and pubs separately. If you had to think of a place where members of both of these divided communities mixed, it was in hospital rooms. We all came into that divided city – walled, built on the oak-fringed banks of the River Foyle – together, and we all left in the same way, no matter which side of the water we had our roots. Derry, the city I was born in and now live in again, is a mostly Catholic city. It was severely affected by the Troubles between 1968 and the Good Friday Peace Agreement of 1998. The actual conflict is widely accepted to have started in this city – right inside its beating heart, in a Catholic residential area known as the Bogside.

Catholics had started to become increasingly unhappy with the preferential treatment being given to the Protestant, mostly unionist, members of society. Jobs and housing – the basics of human rights – were hugely different depending on your surname, and people had had enough. The 1960s, with all its focus on equality, hit the city of Derry hard. No one could really have imagined what would come out of it all though. That is, no one except those who had been living through poverty, inequality and imposed foreign rule. Peaceful marches turned into violent carnage. The RUC, the Protestant police force in the North back then, were filmed beating people – Catholics – with batons. Things escalated: loyalists from the Protestant side attacked housing rights protesters and the police stood by and watched. Catholic men – residents of the Bogside – were beaten to death by the police and died in the only hospital we have, their deaths caused by the only police force we have, the one that was supposed to protect them. The residents of the Bogside swore to never allow the police to enter the estate again. Things began to go from bad to worse.

Paramilitary groups were now operating on both sides of Northern Ireland's sectarian divide, while these essential civil rights marches became increasingly dangerous to attend. In the middle of all this tension, the Protestant, unionist Orange Order's marching season had begun. Following the annual Apprentice Boys' march in August 1969, civil unrest in Belfast became a three-day explosion of nationalist rioting in Derry.

The 'Battle of The Bogside', three days of serious violence in this housing estate, resulted in the arrival of a small body of British troops. What the media across the water were telling us was that the government of Northern Ireland was fast losing its grip on security. We didn't need them to tell us that we were not safe.

A blizzard of reforms came along, including the setting up of a variety of bodies to allocate council housing, to investigate the violence and review policing. The findings made it clear that things were not working and needed to change. This was not the story that had been told in the North of Ireland for many years. The old lore was no longer holding sway, and nothing could ever again be how it once had. Outraged loyalists responded with yet more civil unrest and violence, attacks on Catholic areas escalated, and many homes were burned.

In late 1969, the more militant 'Provisional' IRA broke away from the 'Official' IRA. This group was prepared to pursue unification of the island of Ireland, and would use violence to tear the unwanted border up from the land and the sea, to throw it back over the water, back to where it was sent from.

At the same time, loyalist paramilitaries were also organising. The Ulster Volunteer Force was joined by the Ulster Defence Association, which rapidly expanded to a membership of tens of thousands.

In the middle of it all was the British Army. There was by this stage no hope of stopping the violence that had spilled out of the cracks in the North of Ireland, the sharpest and most splintered shards of which had buried themselves in my hometown of Derry, right on that invisible, contentious border.

At the end of January in 1972, the army deployed the Parachute Regiment to deal with rioting at another civil rights march in Derry. The protest, like all of them, had been peaceful. The footage – almost unbearable to watch – along with eyewitness reports, shows hands being held up, of obedience and fearful fleeing, as those in charge act in a way that might only be termed as unimaginably inhumane. Thirteen demonstrators were shot and killed by troops, with another person dying later from their wounds. 'Bloody Sunday' will go down in the history of this city as one of its most horrific, traumatising and haunting days. The loss, confusion, fear and anger that sparked out of the fires of that harrowing day resulted in 'direct rule' – Northern Ireland would be governed from Westminster. It has remained that way ever since, even with devolution, in the eyes of many, when push comes to shove.

·

I was born into the middle of this violence, at its exact midway point: 1983. Although no one could have known it, on that cold winter's day in Derry. No one has even an inkling, back then, but they are halfway through those dark years. They are over the hump of the hill. The violence that has been filling their every waking day, their every sleepless night, will be brought to an end. The kidnapping and terrorising, the bombing and burning, the mauling and murdering, is not going to last for ever. We do not know yet the journey that the land on which we live, and all of us who live on it, will make. We do not yet know the lengths and breadths, the words and actions, the negotiating that will be required to take us from being a land of violence to a land of (more or less) peace. Some of us, in fact, may never know the ins and outs of this process, our journey towards peace in the North of Ireland, our Peace

Process. We will not know of the words whispered between people, between humans that had never broken breath to one another before. We may never know of the bargains and sacrifices made, of the leaps of something – something unthinkable – that were taken. Leaps of something that feels much stronger, even, than sheer 'faith'. That border has seen it all – every last trace of the violence, bloodshed, silence, trust – the peace that has been carefully and sensitively shaped. A peace as delicate as the wings of a moth.

My grandfather was born in the same week as the Irish border. He was a storyteller, and his most affecting tales, the ones he gave me that have shaped my life, were about *place*, about how we relate to it, to ourselves, and to one another. Good *seanchaidhthe* – storytellers – never really *tell* you anything, though. They set the fire in the hearth; they draw the chairs in close; they shut all the windows so the old lore doesn't fall on the wrong ears. They fill the room with a sense of ease, a sense of all being as it should be. The words, when they spill quietly out of the mouth of the one who has been entrusted with them, dance in the space, at one with the flames of the fire. It is, as always, up to those who listen to do with them what they will.

The stories he shared were fleeting, unbidden; they came and went as quickly as the bright, defiant end sparks of a fire, well on its way to going out. The stories, those glowing embers of words, were about places that are known to hide away, sometimes from all view. As if their locations are to be found in between the cracks, or floating above the thick grey Atlantic.

Places that he mostly didn't even have names for but that he could conjure up as though they were right there in the same room. He called such places 'skull of a shae'. Now, I have come to think of the shae as 'shade', a nod to the almost ghost-like nature he saw such places as having. The places he spoke of seemed to scare him, a wee bit, or maybe it was talking about them that unsettled him. He came from a strict and hard background that allowed very little room for the voicing of much beyond the grind of being alive. I will remember, always, how he spoke of paths, particularly ones he found when walking across the border from Derry into Donegal. Paths on which friends and he had seen and heard things they were never really able to understand.

The places he spoke of were locations where people felt very different from how they normally do. Places from which people came away changed. In these places you might experience the material and spiritual worlds coming together. Blood, worry and loss might sit together under the same tree as silence, stillness and hope. He spoke, not often but with raw honesty, of places where people had found answers and grace, where they had learned to forgive, where they had made peace and room for healing. Places where a veil is lifted away and light streams in, where you see a boundary between worlds disappear right before your eyes, places where you are allowed to cross any borders, where borders and boundaries hold no sway. Lines and circles, silence and stillness – all is as it should be for that flickering gap in time. He never named the places, of course, and the first time he brought me to one – Kinnagoe Bay – on a soft, pink August afternoon in the late 1980s, he never spoke of any of this at all. He quietly read his magazine about pigeon racing, poured my granny's tea, and let me be.

This August in 2019, decades after that first experience with a thin place in my grandfather's company, just days after I returned from another thin place across the water, British politics reached what may go down in history as one of its darkest days.

•

I was in the Waterside in Derry. I was in the border town I grew up in, one that has, in recent years, found itself caught up in a spiralling chaos of Brexit negotiations that seem as if they will never settle. That August afternoon almost half a year ago, I was by the fire in my rented house, caught between two heavy showers of Atlantic rain. The BBC shared with us all that the government had asked the Queen to suspend Parliament. It was only a handful of weeks before the Brexit deadline, October 2019 – the date on which, for three years, we had been told the UK would leave the EU. We had no idea then – not a single one of us – how any of the coming weeks, months or years would look for the islands of the United Kingdom. The single issue that has caused – and is still causing – unrivalled difficulty, is the question of the Irish border. Almost every politician has been able to agree on one thing – there is never going to be an easy way out of this mess when it comes to that invisible line.

We are all standing together looking out at an unknowable thing. Some of us already know what that utter terror, that dark and traumatising uncertainty, feels like. Some of us have lived through things on the same level – rather, some of us have already *survived* such times. Some of us who grew up during the unsettled, devastating – horrifying – Troubles feel those ripples on our insides start to move again. Some of us left at the first chance we got, and we never looked back. Some of us stayed – following the paths of our parents and our peers – never learning another way, steering our ships always towards the same violence and anger that we knew and understood, keeping the same wounds open from the past that nearly broke us. Some of us, though, some of us ran away, and then – somehow – found a way back. Now we watch from the sidelines in horror. The North of Ireland voted against leaving the EU in the referendum of 2016. Our votes mattered not a single jot. Our peace – worth more than anyone can verbalise – is in the hands of people who act as though we do not even exist. Who is to say we will not again witness atrocities the kind of which we have already seen, if we matter as little as we did back then?

•

On a wet night last month, in October 2019 – a few months after the suspension of Parliament by Boris Johnson, a handful of weeks before the UK was due to leave the EU – I went into my concrete backyard in search of the only patch of cloudless sky, in search of stars.

Earlier that day, before the rain had properly set in, I'd gone for a run. Instead of running my usual route – along the River Foyle to look for the same herons and lapwings, the same light on the same reeds – I felt compelled to run a different route in the park. The news that day was so harrowing, full of politics that seemed to grow darker by the hour.

I took my anxious body a different path. I made my way around the football pitch instead of along the stream, up a hill with empty energy drink cans and one discarded stiletto, into a wee copse. Burnt grass and shards of glass from Tesco own-brand vodka bottles, no light to be found at all. And then she came, wild and beautiful, in flight in the least likely of settings – a mottled brown and white moth. I followed her path above broken glass bottles – things that speak of the addiction and poverty that are already here, which looks like it will worsen in the future that lies ahead. Broken things that spoke of our need. Then she was above a dash of red – the first fairy ring I had ever seen in Ireland. Later, before the night fell, I looked her up and found that she was an Oak Beauty. She is very specific to this wooded, broken city of mine. Even as I thought I was open of mind and eye, the moth that afternoon told me to come closer still, tells me – even now – that all is not lost in this place, not yet.

Nature is not somewhere we go into. Nature is not just 'my' river, or the tundra, the highlands, an island, an empty beach or a perfectly sculpted woodland. Nature is not always silent and a bringer of healing. It is not for any one type of person, with any particular background. Nature is the burnt grass that birthed those almost unreal fly agaric, that fairy ring. It is that moth as she jolted me out of my (creeping in) small-mindedness, and desire to box her off. It is the humans of my hometown who are responding to trauma through addiction: the human desire to feel numb sometimes, to ease the worry and the pain, and the sadness, just for a wee while. I hope that the moth danced for them, too – whoever drank and smashed those bottles – and that they noticed her.

Slowly, that autumn night, burning through the grey fog, the stars appeared. Then, under the stars, close enough that I could feel it in my bones, there was a loud deep shot. Then a siren. I awoke the next morning to find out that the sound was a bomb, one street over from mine.

I am not ready for this again, none of us are. I blustered about the house, sinking into the depths, a place I cannot bear to reach again. I can't live through it again, that much I know.

I watched a spider pushing her eggs from the shower switch to the crack in the corner of the bathroom ceiling, slowly, with intention – the egg sac the same colour as a robin's egg, the same colour as my eyes after crying.

I lit the fire, cursing the storm that raged outside on that afternoon, head full of worry about the melting, the burning, the breaking, full of guilt at my part in it all. The flames had seemed almost to dance in time with the howling winds that were shoving the trees around outside, and I remember how comforted I felt by it, by the fact that the winds still howl, and that I still love them, despite it all. It is still there, that breaking and bruising – that sorrow and deep, dark ache – but

I am listening now, with everything I have. I am trying to find the way through.

•

At the age of eight Beatrix Potter was already studying and recording a wide variety of creatures in a sketchbook she herself had made. She was particularly drawn to the delicate form of insects, becoming a keen amateur entomologist at a young age. Potter made frequent visits to the Natural History Museum to sketch their insect collection. Then she would return home, where she learned to prepare slides of specimens to view under a microscope.

At the age of eight in February 1992, I heard, in very hushed voices, the news of a mass shooting in Belfast. Members of the UDA, a loyalist paramilitary group, opened fire, killing five people and wounding another nine. All the victims were local Catholic civilians. Less than an hour after this, my dad's 'Video Van' – our family's sole source of income on our impoverished Protestant housing estate – was driven through British army checkpoints. My father was at the wheel of the van, under the enforced direction of armed loyalist paramilitaries. He has never to this day spoken to anyone about the words the unwanted passengers said to him. About how it felt to be told what to do, where to drive, by someone carrying a loaded gun; someone who could take your life at any moment they chose. When he made it home, nothing felt like it had before he left. Nothing has ever felt the same since.

I knew something bad had happened because my dad didn't go out that night in the van. He didn't go out again for quite a long time. My memories of that year are fairly hazy, as things went from bad to worse politically in Derry, but I do know that in that same year, at the same age as Beatrix Potter, I too was given my own microscope. Suddenly, in that concrete 'garden' on a council estate in a city tearing itself to shreds, another world opened itself up, and let me come in.

I hope you never find yourself in a situation where you need to protect a child from witnessing bloodshed in the very streets on which they have no choice but to live. But if you ever should, I urge you, find books about wild creatures for them, find them a microscope, a magnifying glass, anything at all that helps the unknown make sense. It doesn't matter how broken the surroundings may be, how bombed-out, how terrifying every single bit of it all may be. Just find them a way to sit in muck, as creepy-crawlies do their do, as bees buzz through holes in concrete walls, as spiders build webs on empty coal bunkers under a sky that − no matter how grey and uncertain − holds room for butterflies, moths, dragonflies and things too hard to find words for.

Every February I have dreams of the February I have just recounted. *This* February, during a fierce Atlantic storm, I took my own van from Derry along the coastline, across that border of increasingly tumultuous clamour, to Sligo. When I awoke from a night of dreaming *in* a van, I had not dreamed *of* a van. I only remember one dream from that stormy night, and it was both surreal and deeply moving in equal measure.

In the dream I was living in a previous home and I had a shelf full of found objects from wild places. There were seed pods, mermaid purses and a row of the roundest pebbles imaginable. There were shells the shapes of which were so daedal it was as if they had been sculpted in another world. There were fragile, hollow bones, bleached white over centuries. But the most beautiful object of all, that shelved article which I have not yet shaken out from my mind, months later, was a dead butterfly.

It had been laid atop the wood exactly as it had been found, its wings folded over on themselves, like the painted versions we used to make at school. Do you remember? The teacher would hand you a perfectly symmetrical paper creature and let you place little dots of paint all over one wing only. Next you would fold the other wing over upon the first, gently massaging the liquid paint. And next, the waiting game: would yours be as beautiful as the real-life ones? Never, of course, could this have been the case. The dream butterfly, like the painted, mirror ones from our childhoods, had folded in upon itself but its exquisite markings could still be made out on those fragile wings. It was the most understated shade of brown – full of autumn, with splashes of furry burnt orange, like leaves on top of drying mulch. On the underside of the hind wing, there was a curve of small spots that looked like eyes. Right at the point I saw the eyes, the creature unfolded itself, slowly and with such delicacy, and flew off the shelf, encircling me, leaving me in no doubt whatsoever of its real state of existence. She was a beautiful – and very much living – Large Heath butterfly.

I awoke to the sound of apocalyptic rain battering the van roof, as if the land were in battle. I drove further along the Wild Atlantic Way as the storm threw horizontal sheets of rain down onto the grey, swollen world. In the early evening, when a phone signal could be had, I logged into Instagram to find my feed full of insects of every type – a collective response to a devastating article the *Guardian* had just published about rapid insect decline, full of heart-wrenching, panicking truths. A handful of hours after a dream in which an insect thought dead proved to be alive, I read the news that within a century they could ALL be gone. How are we meant to go on from here? The only thought I had was: *I have no words*. Not in the way that the teenagers around me '*literally can't even*' but in the way of: *I am living on my home island, on the soil of my ancestors, and I don't even have the word for butterfly in my native language.* It began to seep in then. The loss of the ability to name both the landscape and the creatures we share it with in Irish began to sink in. An incomparable loss has been touching the wider world, growing with each news report we hear, during my lifetime. Somehow I had always viewed that loss of wild things as being unrelated to the loss in my homeland, as though they could not really be spoken of in the same breath. But I started to feel an ache, a deep sorrow, when I began to see it all in the clear light of day. How interconnected, how finely woven every single part of it all was. In Ireland, the loss we experienced has had a rippling impact on our sense of self and our place in the world, which has its impact on our ability to speak out, to protect, to name. Our history, our culture, our land, our identity: we have had so much taken away from us – we were never given any of it back.

For the first time properly in a long time, I felt the loss of things, of precious things – the loss of things I realised I could not even name.

Moths and butterflies hold more than unrivalled beauty on their wings, though; they act as indicators of so much within our world. Almost everything can be looked at more deeply through the study of moths and butterflies: birth, genetics, death and more. The words 'fragile' and 'delicate' are often used when we talk about these graceful, beauteous insects but when I think of them I am taken by their inherent ability to endure, by the strength that a creature so small must hold within itself in order to traverse such distances across time and place. I hold them in my mind as creatures bathed in resilience, brimming with wonder.

In old Irish folklore, butterflies were the souls of the dead and it was unlucky to harm one. The Red Admiral butterfly, however, was thought to be the devil and was persecuted. The idea of the butterfly as the embodiment of the soul implies their ability to cross into the Otherworld. My ancestors often saw no boundary at all between wild places and that Otherworld which we cannot see.

•

After university, I left Ireland at the very first chance I got and moved 'across the water' – first to Edinburgh, then Bristol –

desperate to strip away all the layers of trauma that a childhood of devastating violence had left in its wake. I was drawn to the wildest parts of that neighbouring island – highlands and islands, forests and woods, bodies of water of every shape and form. Those parts of the land and water became a form of refuge for me, a way of getting through.

I'm not really sure if it was a conscious thing exactly, this seeking out of special places, like the ones my grandfather spoke of. Out of all my broken-up, aching family, he was the one who offered me constancy and guidance. When he called me on the landline every Sunday evening, the first thing he asked me was if I'd gone anywhere over the weekend. If I'd got outside the flat – outside Dublin, Cork or Edinburgh – what he was really asking was if I'd found somewhere I could feel outside the past. There could be no doubt about it what-soever: the Sunday evenings when I *had* managed to drag myself out into the natural world – to beaches and rivers, loughs and canals, fields and islands – everything felt different. I don't know if I could honestly say that things felt better but I think that maybe I felt a little more at ease with the sorrow and anxiety that I was struggling to throw off. Slowly, and with very little consciousness of what I was doing, I began to take myself into places where vast but quiet shifts took place in me.

I don't know if such places as Grianan of Aileach, Treshnish on the Isle of Mull, Mwnt cove on the Ceredigion coast or the Cornish Merry Maidens have a name in any other language. I don't know if anyone else refers to these places as being 'skull places', or 'places of shade'. I don't know if my grandfather ever spoke of them to anyone else; he never did once in my company. I have never, and never will, google the term gifted to me by my grandfather. Some things are best left as they are. In Ireland, these places are often referred to as *áiteanna tanaí, caol áit* – thin places.

Heaven and earth, the Celtic saying goes, are only three feet apart, but in thin places that distance is even shorter. They are places that make us feel something larger than ourselves, as though we are held in a place between worlds, beyond experience. After years of visiting such places *away* from Ireland, I heard a voice calling me back, a soft but insistent cry: a call back to my own *áiteanna tanaí*.

A call back to the land that made me, that wounded and broke me, the land that turned out to be the only place that held the power for me to heal. A call back to places that I know my grandfather sought out, and maybe his grandfather before him, too.

Some places are ports in what can be – for many people – a life both unsettled and stormy, spaces in which you can leave that which is familiar, all that you hold to be true, and move closer to all that is unknown. Closer to what some may view as the divine, the otherworldly: that which is rooted in something both constant, yet continuously ebbing and flowing. They are in many ways a form of stopping place, liminal space that feels like it has been set aside for silence and deep, raw solitude. To carve out room within ourselves – unintentionally, even – to imagine what lies beyond the here and the now. Places where the veil is thin allow for pauses in the flow of what we know – or think we know – of time. A place to imagine what it all might mean, how we have been, how we maybe *could* be – a space to more clearly see a way through.

The lives each of us has lived is ours alone. Our trauma and suffering, our joys and hopes are ours alone, no matter who we may have shared them with. The things that we need to help us get by are, of course, just as individual. There are as many ways to try to heal a wound as there are paths through a housing estate, forest, coastline or corridor. For some of us, place is one of those lines in the tarmac – a clearing in the brambles, a lighthouse, safe harbour. Places that anchor, nurture and hold us do not have to be beautiful, cut-off, or even what might be described as wild. I'm not just talking about forests, mountains and wild coves. I am also thinking about supermarket car parks with even just one tree, the back of housing estates where life has been left to exist, dump-piles in burnt-out factories where insects glisten, dirty streams at the edges of things – full of waste but still brimming with something like renewal. Places can be abandoned, dangerous, rugged or broken – haunted by the ghosts of dark memories – but still they might help us find a way through, a sense of safety – even just for a little while. There is so much life in the places around us and, sometimes, for some of us, somehow, this helps us to value our own life. Maybe even at times when the act of staying alive is a daily struggle.

Battles, governments, laws, leaders – borders – come and go, but the land and its sacred places remain unmoved and unchanged in their core. There are some places in this broken, burning and bleeding world in which I have experienced moments – fleeting but clear as winter light – where I feel hope like the beat of moth-wings on my skin. There are still places on this earth that sing of all that came and left, of all that is still here and of all that is yet to come. Places that have been touched, warmed, by the presence of something. By its heat, by its breath, by the beat of its heart. Places that hold on their surface a shadow-trace left behind by something we can still sense but no longer see.

## CHAPTER TWO

## *The Bridge of Sorrows*

EVEN AS A CHILD, I could see no way of staying in my hometown. The edges of the broken and breaking city never quite held themselves in place, and my own family life mirrored those fractures. There was just so much loss all around me. Everywhere I turned seemed stabbed right through, constantly punctured by the outside world. The past, present and future all seemed to blend into one, and every single part of the story held sorrow that I couldn't get rid of, no matter how deep I tried to bury it. So many different things – situations, times of year, people – made the bad things rise up from inside to bite me again. Triggers, I know that now. It left me feeling scared, hollowed out and with no control over any of it, not really knowing how to make it – any of it – stop.

I grew up, to start with, in a terraced house on a rough grey council estate. Rather, I started my growing up in the garden of that house, spending as much time knee-deep in the mud that never really dried out due to the unstoppable rain that swept in from the Atlantic. Ours is a past steeped in rust, a history bathed in thick black squelch, mudlarking, always, for our sense of self.

If I had to describe that first house I would struggle. I remember a yellow teapot on the top shelf of a chipped red dresser in the kitchen, which looked out onto the garden. If on the other hand you asked me to describe that small space enclosed by tall grey concrete walls, filled with the sounds of the next-door neighbours fighting through windows that wouldn't close properly, I could outline that garden for you in perfect and minute detail. I spent most of my early child-hood, no matter the season, in that man-made jungle of a garden. I was outside every chance I got. I was outside because it simply made no sense to me to be indoors. My parents would find me, utterly transfixed and bogging dirty, hands holding all sorts of treasure. I'd beg them to close their eyes and open their grown-up hands so I could fill them with the wonder of the living, breathing, dying world. Broken bricks in the corner of the back yard filled up with ladybirds in descending size order, each limb and wing compared and contrasted against its brother or sister. Frogs would come to our garden from the stream at the bottom of our housing estate to die and I buried each one with a handwritten poem. I grieved for them so deeply, so fully; I remember feeling their loss like a wounded knee. During those early days in our housing estate's concrete, impoverished world I learned so much about just getting through. I didn't realise this for many decades though, and it took me many more years of growth to understand that sometimes, out of concrete cracks, hardy, bright poppies appear in places where no seed has been planted.

Back then, the city of Derry had seen twenty years of civil war in its public spaces – our sacred and safe places – which had resulted in a deep-rooted fear, the ripples of which could be felt in more than just the devastating human loss that was visible. When whole streets are burned down, and the face of a city changed beyond recognition, very few folk notice their disconnect with the natural world. When you've no home to go to because it's been petrol bombed, seeking the wonder of the wild world is not a priority. Derry was a dark city to be in for my childhood and I was scared. That first housing estate was completely Protestant. As a child I knew the disgusting words being thrown around my street as loosely as lemonade-bottle petrol bombs were about Catholics just like my mum. I knew everything could go up in smoke at any moment, as you were walking to buy credit to feed the 'poverty bells' – the squealing electricity meter.

The worse things got in our council estate – children being suffocated with flags for being from the wrong street, punishment beatings, cats being burned within inches of their lives as a warning to their unwelcome owners – the more I retreated into myself. I stopped talking and would sit at the bottom of our garden alone, facing the grey plaster wall for hours. I grew wordless – trapped under the weight of the violence, silently screaming out from under the frozen river.

Loss and violence swallowed the verges of things and I watched from the corner as my childhood was eaten up. The shadow that my hometown made of itself – and of all those still held within – left no space for anything else, there was too much darkness to even try to grow. The Troubles have left scars that run too deep to see. I left at the earliest point I could, but none of those new places gave me the feeling of home I was so desperately searching for. I wore loss and sorrow on the surface of my weathered young skin. I ran from place to place, rootless, lonely, and never quite knowing how to ask anyone to help me back up from underneath the hard black ice.

Time, as we know, like the sea, is a force and a creature all of its own. We can stop neither of them. We stand on the sand, watching as the days become years, as the line made by the tide disappears, as the hungry waves devour the borderline that once defined the land. People, places, experiences and the act of living a life, our days come together and we find we have grown; we are being carried in time's salty course. I found myself, a third of the way through the year that was 2016, at the age of thirty-one, returning to my hometown of Derry, doing the one thing I'd promised myself I would never, ever do.

I had spent my teens and all of my twenties absolutely desperate to get away, to pretend I was the same as other people my age, who hadn't lived through what I had, who weren't carrying things the like of which I was still carrying and feeling like I had to pretend weren't there. When I look back now I see that it was much more about embarrassment and an inexplicable sense of shame than it was about the past itself. We all became – many of us did, anyhow – so set on trying to gloss over it all, those violent, terrifying memories, so keen to try to make sure none of it ever came back. It felt a wee bit like being a child again and again and again. Did you ever spend days obsessed with the idea of your loved ones dying, your house burning down, your favourite toy or book being stolen, and the only way to stop any of it, to make sure it didn't happen, was not to step on the cracks on the pavement? To hold your breath until you reached the bottom stair. If it was only red cars that passed your window then everything would be okay, nothing bad would happen that day at all. If I played it all down, just gave one or two small, inconsequential details of my childhood – if I kept enough of it back that it was at least slightly believable – it'd all be fine. If I didn't have to keep saying how fine I was – how *it was grand, sure; so many people had been through so much worse;* and *sure, hadn't I got so lucky* – then I would fade into the background. I wouldn't risk feeling that I was being pitied, doubted, viewed as a damaged and broken thing.

Every time something new happened to fill my life with worry and pain, or an old wound was forcibly reopened, it felt too ridiculous to even try to share it with those I had built a new life around. It wasn't that my friends and colleagues were not caring and supportive people; they very much were, and still are. It was just that sometimes even the explanations are too much to bear. So I tried to deal with it all myself, not in any selfless way, but because I had no coping skills that would allow me to let those around me step in close, close enough that they could try to understand the way it all fitted together, the way my present was weighed down by a past that wouldn't go away.

I'd been struggling silently for well over a decade to find the courage to resurface from under the frozen river, to let the light flood into the parts that scared – and scarred – me to my core. At the time I told no one how badly I was feeling. That I felt sick when I thought of myself, when I thought of my past. I told no one that – grateful though I was for so much in my life – most days the overriding feeling was still helplessness, and paralysing hopelessness, too. That almost every single day I felt like the only way out was really *out*, out of the life I was in . . . and I could see only one way to do that. Suicidal thoughts are incredibly hard to bury, no matter how you might try. Back then, most days, in the early morning light, the only thing stopping me from taking my own life was guilt. Even now I tell very few people the whole truth of how my mental health has looked over the last two decades. Depression is still something many of us suffer in deepest silence.

That solid body of icy water casts quite a spell. Those who have grown up with deep trauma can drown underneath it. From the age of sixteen onwards, at differing levels of intensity, I experienced suicidal thoughts that I found increasingly hard to cope with as the years went by. I felt, through both of the decades between then and now, that the only chance I stood of making it through was by staying away from where I came from. To stay away from the place where I'd lived through things that I could not even begin to process. I swore that I was never ever going back to Ireland. The worse things got the harder I swore. That city I grew up in would drown me. That city would kill me, of that I was utterly sure.

And then, one day, just as my thirties had begun, something vast broke inside me. I began to wake up every single morning feeling like I was being called back. I could hear the land trying to say my name, a thing I never imagined I would ever hear, and I could not ignore it. It came unbidden, all out of nowhere, and nothing was the same after I began to feel drawn back to this place. I awoke most mornings for close to a year with the streets of Derry mapped out on the insides of my very being, a morphed and unwarranted cartography.

Every corner I turned in my adopted home across the water transformed itself right before my confused eyes — becoming Shipquay Street, The Diamond, Carlisle Road, Fahan Street. I was being enshrouded by the geography of a city many miles across the sea. I was being haunted by places I thought had long been abandoned and buried far beneath my feet. I couldn't — no matter how hard I tried — in the deadness and in the fullness of the night, get the view from the top of the *Grianán Ailigh* out of my head. The light of Inch Island on a frosty morning; a *Faoilleach* — winter — storm coming into rest on Kinnagoe Bay; whooper swans in a delicate V above the River Foyle. The harrowing memories were resurfacing, too, but they were no longer coming on their own. Something had changed. I was letting it all come to the surface. I had lifted my own veil, the one that had hidden things away for decades — things that I needed, more than anything else in the world, to finally look in the eye.

I felt the violence and sorrow from my past creeping up my guts, clawing to get out – and I didn't know what I was supposed to do. I knew I had to let it surface, at long last, but how was I expected to cope? Fear covered over everything, leaving my thoughts coated with a blank whiteness I could never quite shake off. I didn't know what would be left underneath – how my relationship with my homeland would look when that snow melted away. If I went back to where my faultlines were forged, would there be a new outline? Would I see beyond the sorrow – down deeper?

I gave in. More simply than that, I gave. I was the thing that had to give. I returned to Derry, ready to try to translate those words. Those words that had begun to thaw out after decades of fearful silence.

There is a power to place – a hold that is kept over us – a woven thread that never really loosens itself once we have been there, and been held by it. I didn't realise until very recently the impact that the spaces I had sought refuge in as a child could, and would, continue to have on me as an adult. The ripples of geography continue to be traced on our inner surfaces, even if our experience there was fleeting and seemed like nothing to us at the time. No matter how long ago the experience was, its power, its healing, sits in wait, sometimes buried deep, other times just waiting to be called back from within.

When I returned to Derry, after living away for almost my entire adult life, I found that I was drawn back again and again to very particular geographical spaces. Often these were places that I hadn't even realised were of any deep importance or meaning to me. I also assumed, for some reason, that when I moved back, the longing I felt for places – for exact spots in particular parts of my city and island – would ease, dissipate even. I assumed that the overwhelming yearning, so extreme as to be almost a physical sensation, for *places* would leave me once I lived on Irish soil once more. As of yet, it hasn't left me. I feel it almost like a hunger. A hunger to be in the sea at Carrowhugh on the Inishowen Peninsula, even on the iciest days of December. To be at the outermost tip of Inch Island in heavy and battering rainfall. To sleep in my van, held within the very centre of Ireland's beating heart, moving through the bog-land like a curlew. I have started to understand that even when standing barefoot on the soil of my homeland, swimming in any of its bodies of water, heart-deep in the caves, I am still being called back.

It is three and a half years now since I moved home, in a moment that was right on the cusp of the biggest storm to rock the island since the Troubles – the Brexit vote. We are, I fear, in the very eye of the storm. All around me shops lie empty, car bombs have started to go off again on our doorsteps, EU funding has already been pulled out of youth groups, addiction units and much more, even before the UK has officially left the EU. It is weeks yet until the General Election. Already the young folk in Derry stand even less chance of getting on in life than they did before this chaos took hold – chaos we didn't ask for.

Where is our government in Northe[rn]    representation? Where is our voice? One    our Assembly has not sat for three years is beca[use]    over the Irish language. When Martin McGuinness s[tood]    down as Deputy First Minister of Northern Ireland in January 2017 after holding the post for almost a decade, failure to introduce legislation on the Irish language was listed as one of the reasons he effectively ended the Executive. Sinn Féin support the restoration of Irish as the spoken language amongst the majority of people on the island of Ireland. Some unionists are worried as they see the desire for an Irish language Act as a tool to be used by the opposition in a quest for a united Ireland. Place-names in the North of Ireland, as well as the South, come from a variety of sources; however, the vast majority derive from Irish. The desire to cover over this layer of identity, to try to erase our past, is a sign of much more than an unstable political landscape. It also speaks volumes about Ireland's terrifying loss of connection with the natural world: our unwilding. We have already lost so much, and many of the differences perceived between people are associated with language and our link with the land itself. Simple choices – to learn Irish, to try to explore parts of the history of the land that might not necessarily be deemed relevant to 'your side' – can be viewed as weightier than they really are. When I changed my surname back to its Irish original, long before I returned to Ireland, I felt as if it was one of the bravest decisions I had ever made given the reactions I knew I would receive from many people. Many of the things that we have ught over in the past, now that peace has arrived, have been swept away under the carpet for fear that disagreements and fighting might rear their ugly heads again.

The natural world, and our role as guardians – one so linked with the Celtic identity of our ancestors – is one also intrinsically linked with the language of this land. There is wisdom held within the Irish language, knowledge not yet lost to us, but equally as at risk right now as the creatures it has been speaking of for millennia. The Irish language is rooted in a world in which the unseen is as real as the seen. The existence of other dimensions is taken as a given, and there is an inherent understanding that both the land and everything in the natural world are bright, breathing beings. The interconnectedness of things is visible in the etymology: concepts that seem disparate are shown as delicately woven together; we see that we are not as standalone as we might have once believed. The most affecting words I have learned are a tightly knit trinity, and their closeness, for me, shows how unspoken things still dwell in the root of the Irish language, waiting to be unearthed, dissected. *Dúlaoisc* – a sea-level cave; *dúluachair* – the depths of midwinter; and *dúléim* – a leap in the dark, a violent jump, a plunge. I see these connected with fierce, fine thread. There are stories behind these words, human voices that have known suffering. It comes to me as no shock at all that the Irish word for melancholy is *dúlionn*. Language is narrative. The Irish language holds stories that, once excavated, may show us the way that things are tied to others. It offers us, through the language of the everyday, a way to communicate, for example, that some days, even at the height of summer, might be the exact shade of grey as a sea-cave in the depths of midwinter. Communication – real, deep and honest connection – might help to keep us back from that place that makes us want to jump in the dark.

In the North of Ireland we are once more in a state of limbo when it comes to our identity, our heritage, our past and our future. We are being told that, despite the much-fought-for Good Friday Agreement, we are, suddenly, no longer Irish. There is a chance that we will once more see a hard border put in place on the land, to divide, again, the North and South of Ireland. The peace that was so hard won is now more endangered than it has been for years. We have no idea what will come about for us if the Good Friday Agreement – the deal made in the 1990s that brought the worst of the Troubles to an end – is disrespected any further than it already has been. Dissident republicans have already erupted in full and terrifying force. A young journalist, Lyra McKee, was shot dead during a night of rioting in the city. The rioters used the presence of police in Catholic housing estates as an excuse for their violence. Lyra was caught up in this violence as she was doing her job, a vital job, that of ensuring that the truth of the situation here reaches the world. She used her voice to raise issues that affected our generation – 'ceasefire babies' – and showed respect and openness in her work. The night she died she was making sure that those in power, those who hold a vote, those who have spent years blinkered, unaware of the debris that has been left behind on this island, might finally open up their eyes. The loss of Lyra, a young woman full of hope and deep understanding of human nature, and such an inspiring compassion for her homeland and its people, has filled our collective hearts with that same pain from the past. We were not ready for this to begin again. Now that it has, we are not ready for it to escalate any further.

The helicopters are in the sky again every night. At the start I lay awake – scared and angry. Now, like back then, I have become used to it. I sleep right through, just as I am able to walk past the red, white and blue unionists' flags on my street and the increasingly violent graffiti on both sides of the river. I do not want, again, to become someone who just sleeps through. I do not want to be numbed to suffering again. Enough, already. Enough. Brexit, borders, barriers, identity, real and imagined. Place, the concept of home and representation of it, always massive things, now seem so much *more* important – even critical.

This spring, my closest friend from Derry died. Just after her death my father and I walked through St Columb's Park together. It was the first Monday in May, less than a month after that night of Lyra McKee's murder, the news of which had reached me in the same hour as the news that my friend – one I'd navigated secondary school and university with – had been found dead, alone, in the Dublin flat we had once shared together. It was late afternoon by the time my father and I arrived at the sheltered copse of oaks at the top bend of the woods, high above the train line that runs parallel with the River Foyle. Directly across from the tangled thicket in which we had found ourselves – now barricaded off from those of us who cannot dip and dive like the other woodland creatures – is a vast and terrifying drop known as Devil's Glen.

There is a tattered photograph somewhere of my brother and I standing on the train line directly under this now cordoned-off spot, with tens of feet of a drop beneath us. It was taken by my father before he left our home on that first council estate. The photo was taken back in the days when people walked on the metal, sometimes just moments before a train raced towards them, forcing them to jump into the thicket, falling backwards into nettles, blackberry bushes or wild strawberry patches. The only creatures that can make their way onto that track now are winged ones: butterflies and moths, long-tailed tits and blackbirds, memories and longing.

A handful of hours before the news of the deaths reached my home, I had run along the river from the bottom of the park, alongside reed beds full of long-tailed tits and coot families, right down to the concrete, graffitied beauty of the Foyle Bridge. The sun had been full of promise and I had seen the same heron five times at different points of the river's meandering. Seeing herons always soothes me a little. They are often viewed as an ominous, fearful bird, but I have a deep-rooted fondness for those almost prehistoric-looking waders. Seeing them makes me feel like I am in the right place at the right time, somehow. I see them as a gift from another time.

There are ruins in the park from a church rebuilt on the site in 1585. The original church was destroyed in 1197. When we were children my wee brother and I clambered all over those ruins. We climbed them as if they were a pile of stones we ourselves had placed in the landscape, as though we knew them so well that maybe we had even carved them with our own hands. In those days, things were 'let be', as they say. Bombing, poverty, violence, a sense of the uncontrollable inevitability of things, had resulted in buildings – often histor-ical, ancient – being left to live out the rest of their lives as best they could, unmanaged. I remember the feel of the grey, religious stone under my feet on summer days – never quite hot to touch, but warmed, as though the stone had only just come out of the earth's belly. It might be a bit odd but I like to imagine that there was an invisible footmark of us two wee Derry weans left there on those ruins from all those years ago. I like to imagine the stones as a palimpsest, a trace left behind – layer upon layer – like strata, of all of the children that have ever stood near enough to that church to feel its heartbeat. I want those spaces and places to hold a trace of us all. I want *us* to hold part of those places within our bodies too – I want to believe that we are in this all together – that we are connected. I need to believe that the sea and the land – the places we have been shaped and held by – will show us how to live again, will remind us how to *be*. I need to believe that loss and grief are like stones, too. That they might always remain on our internal landscape but that there is a stillness that comes after, a knowledge that will be left behind – that light will still touch the stone – that we will be held in place despite the storms. There is a beauty to stone that can never quite be forgotten.

My dad and I walked up the hill on that spring day, diverging from the pathway, edging as close to the church as we can now get. It is cordoned-off these days, of course. I am not sure if the council will ever do anything with the site. I could feel its stones call to my heart, but my dad dragged me on with his silence, away from the edges.

•

Despite all of these echoes of my childhood now, there has been much change in the decades held between – change that I am very grateful for. I want to believe that there are enough of us who have had enough. That enough people now care for the future – the future of their home as well as their own lives. That there are enough people within the community now – on both sides – to protect the peace that has been so carefully crafted, the future that finally has the potential to bring positive change for us all. There was more chance of me being able to learn Icelandic than Irish in my childhood in the Waterside of Derry, due to the politics of my hometown (I still speak more Icelandic but I am working hard to redress this balance). I am allowed, finally, to unearth the words. I need to trust that the words are still there. There is a part of me that I will never be able to meet if I do not make efforts to learn the language of my home. That part of me is one for which I think I have been searching for quite some time.

•

On the morning of my thirty-fifth birthday, I woke up to an *Irish Times* newspaper article entitled 'Mass extinction of species is happening in Ireland'. The article stated that a third of the species groups examined are threatened with extinction, predominantly due to global warming, habitat loss, pollution and unsustainable use of resources. A number of species are, in fact, 'critically endangered', and without urgent action being taken immediately, they will simply disappear entirely from this island. That morning, I spent so many hours researching what we have already lost – what we risk losing any day – that I nearly wept with the sadness of it all. Some of those creatures in most danger are the curlew, the European eel, the pearl mussel, the bumblebee, the barn owl, the corncrake and the marsh fritillary butterfly.

Native species that have become extinct over my lifetime include two types of birds: the corn bunting and the corncock. Such a major downturn has taken place in the three and a half decades I have been alive, that almost thirty species of bird and almost five times that number of flowering plants are in serious decline. Over ten vertebrates, over a hundred and twenty invertebrates. Since I was at university native butterflies have decreased by almost half.

Less than two months after the *Irish Times* article, I read another devastating piece about species loss on a wider scale in the *Guardian*. I spent days utterly unable to read or write another single word.

That week I turned the radio on. Gideon Coe was on BBC Radio 6. He was reading a text from a listener in Scotland. I was rapt. The listener had been driving when the distinct feeling that he was sharing the car with something else came over him. Something tickled his ear, his head, his cheek. He batted and shooed at the unseen thing; eventually his unwanted passenger landed on his satnav. The listener said: 'I don't think we will be hearing from the moth again.' Gideon Coe fell silent, as if he could find no way to respond. I sat at my kitchen table utterly aghast, angry, grieving for a moth I had never even seen, killed on a satnav in the car of a man I had never met. I turned the radio off that night, sat in a completely silent kitchen, and wept.

I sat at my kitchen table that satnav moth night and I knew I had to do something – anything – to make me feel like I was actually taking action. Like I was doing something that might make some kind of difference. I took out my phone and the first – the only thing – that I could think of was to find an online Irish translation app. I felt it so fully, for the first time, the link between the past and the future, the land and the language, and my place in it all. I felt stuck in the gaps between these markers of our confused, lost maps. I knew I was not alone; all of us in Ireland are living on a land scarred by much that has been lost, and by much that we must learn how to begin to protect. The hedgerows and rivers, the sea and the mountains, the laneways and stone-scattered bog-land: these are part of us. They are part of our past and our identity. The things that live alongside us have names that many of us do not know, were never taught – and that night I could see it all so clearly. Naming things, in the language that should always have been offered to you, is a way to sculpt loss. A way to protect that which we still have. Naming and language, hand in hand, called to me that night.

I began to look, and to listen; I began to search. I didn't stop searching until my phone battery died. Until I was shattered from the device's blue lights, and from crying. That winter night, almost a year ago, I sat in near darkness flooded by memories from the past. That night, and for some time afterwards, I couldn't quite tie it all up; I couldn't see any thread that connected my thoughts – they felt jumbled and confused, born from grief. Grief so different from that which I already knew. This was collective, overwhelming, inescapable, unstoppable. Eco grief: the knowledge that we have lost so much – creatures, plants and places – that we mostly stand no chance at being able to bring back. The knowledge that the earth has been changed so vastly, so drastically, so fully, that we can never reverse the process. The knowledge that one person cannot stop, change or undo this – any of it – but that we have to choose if we will stand back and watch, or if we will fight. I had known for years that the climate was changing, the earth was being compromised, that our species was putting those we share this planet with at serious risk. But that night something was born in me that has grown and grown. A grief that has multiplied and magnified, that has taken up residence in me, that shares my habitat. I am changed by it, and I am ready for action. This grief settled in beside grief from so many other losses, from so many other stages of my life. Perhaps those of us who have lost so much already cannot help but feel differently about the loss of moths.

The first thing I translated that night was the word 'satnav', mostly out of embittered anger. The Irish words for satnav are: *loingseoireacht satailíte*. The Irish word for the exquisite creature that the caller killed, that winged beauty is *leamhan*. I searched word after word – writing them down on a piece of paper and guessing how to pronounce them as they danced on the paper like lights on rippling water. I've never felt I was allowed to learn, let alone try to speak my own native language. There is not a single member of my family that was ever taught Irish, on either side. The Protestant primary school we were sent to, followed by the grammar school I attended, made the choice not to teach Irish. In the first housing estate we lived on, the Protestant one, a word of Irish being used in any way other than as ridiculing abuse, would have seen you victimised to the point of being put out. When we lived on the Catholic housing estate, Irish was used as a means of ostracising, too. I remember not even knowing if the words being spoken were real Irish, or if the lads from the house across the road were just making them up, testing us with a language that was indecipherable.

When I thought back to the last time I'd heard Irish – the real language – being spoken, the memory came back much quicker and with more depth than I expected. It had been in the summer, around half a year before that night, and the day in question had been full of living moths and butterflies in the summer shadow of Muckish Mountain in the part of Donegal where the Irish language is still on people's tongues. The light there was a kind that I had not really experienced before; the silence was the same. I was making my way along a path cut through the mountain, more or less unchanged for centuries so few are the journeys made through that part of rural Ireland these days. Less than two hundred years ago, this road would have seen so many human travellers it would have been impossible to keep count. The road I was on last summer, the last time I heard Irish being spoken, was a Famine Road: one of many rural Irish tracks laden with loss and sorrow. These tracks carried people from their homes across Ireland – from the impoverished dwellings of their kith and kin – to the boats at the quaysides, in which they would set sail from their homeland for ever. The lucky ones left by foot, traversing paths through the only land they had ever known, on roads that they would never set eyes or feet on again. Roads that will hold the memory of them on their surface for who knows how long still to come.

I stopped at a wee stone bridge beside another vehicle and all of us, the occupants from both cars, stood together beneath a strong white light that seemed to be the root of all the stillness.

The place where I stopped that day, where a couple beside me spoke to one another in soft, lapping Irish, was 'The Bridge of Sorrows'. In my silent kitchen, still reeling from the death of a moth in a stranger's car, I remembered reading about those emigrants who left Ireland long ago in hope of a brighter tomorrow.

Right beside the little stone bridge a plaque reads first in Irish, with this English translation beneath:

*Family and friends of the person leaving for foreign lands would come this far. Here was the separation. This is the Bridge of Tears.*

The silence of the kitchen was nothing in comparison to that stone Famine Bridge. All of a sudden, I could almost hear the solitary curlew that had sung its siren song above me that summer's day. I could see, in the blue light of the radio, all the butterflies that had danced around me in that space, so defined by loss, grief and sorrow seeping down through ancient peat bog into the otherworld. No matter the devastating loss that Donegal has been hit by, that ethereal, beautiful marsh fritillary has, somehow, returned to parts of the bog that are slowly being managed and cared for. I translated that creature in my kitchen, too – from English into the native tongue that I had never felt the loss of before: *fritileán réisc*.

The next day, I bought my first Irish dictionary and started to spend my lunchtimes in Cultúrlann Uí Chanáin, the Irish language centre in Derry. I learned there, through talking to the barista in the café, that in the part of the Gaeltacht where I'd watched the butterflies dancing above the bridge – Cloughaneely – where Irish was, and may still be, spoken with strength, butterflies have a different name. She didn't know what the name was but she was certain it was specific to that area.

I researched for weeks, eventually finding the name. The Donegal bog word for butterfly is *dealan-dé*. It has roots in the word 'fireflaught', and speaks of the phenomenon observed by shirling a stick lighted at the end: a flash of lightning that comes to you from somewhere closer than the sky. The Donegal Gaeltacht word for butterfly, I discover, is the same word as for the Aurora Borealis: the lights that dance so magically in that liminal place between here and there, then and now, this world and the other. Like the marsh fritillary, my ancestors watched the Northern Lights dance above the vast, wild surface of the earth, imagining that the bog itself had birthed both of these breathtakingly beautiful wonders.

I think back to that plaque on the Bridge of Sorrows, on a Famine Road that still holds its losses embedded in its stones. Those marks that spoke of separation and of tears, of an endless, echoing grief. Long before the building of the railway, or modern roads, this was the only real route from that place to Derry, the place I in turn had fled at the first chance I got. Those who made that journey from here into the port of my hometown were bound for England, Scotland, Australia, Canada or America. Those who were not tramping onwards, the friends and family of those who were departing, would have had no expectation of ever seeing their loved one again. The moment of their parting would have borne a kind of loss I am not sure we can fully comprehend today – the loss from your life, without quarrel or other natural cause, of a dearly loved figure, the near death, in a way, of one who may still go on to outlive you, without you ever seeing their face again. I tried to envision all the weeping that hoary bridge had witnessed in its span, silvered, salted and scoured over centuries by bawling winds. By wailing bog winds, and by the *caoineadh* – the keening – that still vibrates like a dirge. That still echoes above the gorse like a tolling omen, a mourners' hymn, knelling above the curlew's nest like a chant. Like a pealing lament born of stone, born of tears.

I, for one, am not ready for any more separation – from the natural world, from those I do not want to lose, from myself and my sense of worth. I know that I am not alone, either. I am not ready to lose another single thing.

We have lost humans, too, so many people have died, or have left through trauma. Some have chosen to end their own lives; they had reached a point they could not see any way back from. Suicide has had an immense impact on my life, and on the lives of many in the North of Ireland. The suicide rate in Northern Ireland is the highest in the UK – over twice what it is in England – and one of the highest in the world. More people have now died through suicide since the Good Friday Agreement than were killed in political violence during the Troubles. Suicide rates in those years, have, in fact, doubled. Of twenty-eight countries that participated in the World Mental Health survey in 2017, Northern Ireland had the highest rate of PTSD. Talking about traumatising experiences, as peace has unfolded, has remained a difficult thing. A culture of silence takes years, perhaps, to break. This year alone, of the six deaths that have touched my life, it is likely that three of those we have lost ended their own lives. The cause of death wasn't shared at the third funeral – that of the closest female friend I have ever had – and it all feels too raw to explore the events that led to her death. She had told me – so many times that I have had to lose count – that she was going to end her life. Every time the words came out, the pain I felt thinking about her suffering, and the worry about what I was meant to do, floored me. I have only recently stopped feeling wracked with guilt at ending our friendship the year before she died. She was one of the people I have loved most in my lifetime, but from the very beginning until its ending it was one of the most abusive relationships I have ever known.

At least two other friends ended their own lives this year, that much I know for certain. One of those struggled with addiction; the other had long been suffering with mental ill health. Both men were gentle, good people who felt the impact of the place where they were raised. The fourth person died of organ failure, resulting from alcoholism. Loss in Northern Ireland, for many people, consists of layer upon layer of despondency and hopelessness – things that are exceptionally hard for one person to shift on their own, just trying to get through.

I think of the loss of our identity, our language, of our traditions and culture: the things we are told make us who we are. I cannot help but see it all tied up together with the same rope. How can we protect ourselves from things that we cannot talk about? How can we protect things that we cannot name?

I hope our Scottish caller, like me, struggles to get that moth out of his head. I hope that he begins to awaken every morning with the 'want' upon him, a hunger for all those things already lost.

I have returned to the site of my trauma and I am allowing the land to hold me in its strong, silent hands. I have found the words for butterflies in my native tongue, and I am drawing their lines on my insides. I am ready, now, to speak of unname-able things. I know that so, so many of us are. To stand together under an ever-changing sky, and to speak of things like healing and learning, the saving of things that can still be saved.

To stand together under a sky that − no matter how grey and uncertain − still holds room for butterflies, moths, dragon-flies and things we once were too fearful to name; things like whispered hope.

The Irish word for hope is *dóchas*, or *dóigh*, and holds, deep within its ancient roots, glimmers of the Irish word for giving, for belonging, for beauty: *dóighiúil*.

Yes, we are ready, now, to speak of *hope*. We have the *words* for it, and that changes things. In fact, that changes *everything*.

# CHAPTER THREE

## *Frozen River*

Wʜᴀᴛ ᴅᴏᴇꜱ ɪᴛ ᴍᴇᴀɴ ᴛᴏ come from a hollowed-out place? From a place that is neck-deep in the saga of loss? What does it mean when your origins trace a line made of leaving – of going away to far away lands – with the knowledge that *this* goodbye was to be the very last on any shoreline that you could touch? What effect does where you come from, and what that land has been through, have on the map of your self? How deeply can a person feel the fault lines of their home running through their own veins?

In Celtic lands it is not unusual to use the landscape as a mnemonic map. Geographical features hold a particular importance for our history, beliefs and culture – places make up the lines of our very being. There is an understanding that we are part of and not separate from the land we inhabit. Celtic legends place the natural world at the very heart of the story, maybe even inside its bones. In such stories things in the natural world can possess a spirit and presence of their own; mountains, rocks, trees, rivers – all things of the land and the sea – sing their own lament. Locations can be associated with a particular warrior, hero or deity. Places are tied to stories by threads that uncoil themselves back beyond known history, passed on through oral tradition, only some of which have been written down.

Amongst these geographical features, whether manmade – such as ancient mounds and standing stones – or naturally created features, it is not unusual for some to be associated with the worship of pre-Christian deities. The *aos sí* (or *aes sídhe*) is an Irish term for a race that is other than human, that exists in Irish, Scottish and Manx mythology, inhabiting an invisible world that sits in a kind of mirroring with our own. They belong to the Otherworld, *Aos Sí* – a world reached through mists, hills, lakes, ponds, springs, loughs, wetland areas, caves, ancient burial sites, cairns and mounds. The island from which I come had no choice, really, than to find a name for these dancing, beating, healing places where the veil between so very many things is thin, where it has been known to lift, right before our humble, grateful eyes.

The folklore of almost every culture holds room for these liminal spaces – those in-between places – those unnamable places, not to be found on any map. Are these thin places spaces where we can more easily hear the land, the earth, talking to us? Or are they places in which we are able to feel more freely our own inner selves? Do places such as these therefore hold power?

We have built up a narrative over many years – decades, centuries? – of 'nature' as 'other'. There is so much separation in the language we use with each other; we seek to divide humanity from its own self again and again, and this has naturally bled into how we view the land and water that we share with one another – and with other species. What do we mean when we talk about 'nature'? About 'place'? I want to know what it all means. I need to try to understand. When we are in a place where the manmade constructs of the world seem as though they have crumbled, where time feels like it no longer exists, that feeling of separation fades away. We are reminded, in the deepest, rawest parts of our being, that we *are* nature. It is in and of us. We are not superior or inferior, separate or removed; our breathing, breaking, ageing, bleeding, making and dying are the things of this earth. We are made up of the materials we see in the places around us, and we cannot undo the blood and bone that forms us.

In thin places people often say they experience being taken 'out of themselves', or 'nearer to god'. The places I return to over and over – both physically, and in my memory – certainly do hold the power to make me feel light and hopeful, as though I am not quite of this world. Of much more power, though, is the way in which these places leave me feeling rooted – as utterly and completely *in* the landscape as I ever feel, as much a part of it as the bones and excrement that lie beneath my feet, as the salt and silt that course through the water. For me, it is in this that the absolute and unrivalled beauty of thin places lies.

Due to the fact that I grew up on a sea and storm-sculpted island, my earliest experiences of thin places involved water.

Being beside water, by a river, waterfall, stream or on a shore-line, carries us into a state of existence neither here nor there. Many people experience water as a nourishing, calming thing, and water features over and over in the history, economy, culture and mythology of Ireland. In Irish mythology rivers and streams are often a boundary between this world and the Otherworld. Ireland's ancient rivers are steeped in tales about the ancient Gaelic gods of the *Tuatha Dé Danann* – the folk of the goddess Danu. The names of many rivers in Ireland are testament to the enduring power of these ancient deities. After the period of Christian conversion in Ireland (from the fourth century CE onwards) the awareness of old pagan deities was not lost. It remained in our stories, traditions and folklore and often merged into tales associated with important figures, and saints linked with the newly arriving religion.

The River Foyle is around eighty miles long. It flows through Lifford, County Donegal, Strabane and County Tyrone. It then flows to the city of Derry, where the Troubles began, then into Lough Foyle and finally out – into the body of the wild Atlantic Ocean.

The river that courses through my hometown shape-shifts at one point in its journey into a rich, silvery lough. A lough that speaks of belonging and of not, a lough that lies, in many ways, in the gaps in between.

The lough was never officially given to either side – North or South – in the Partition of Ireland in 1922, and afterwards both the United Kingdom and the Republic of Ireland claimed it as their territory. In fact, even now, both sides call it their own, although the actual administration of the lough is handled by a joint, cross-border body established under the auspices of the Good Friday Agreement. This lough, then, lies in between the two countries, neither truly of one or the other – a fitting state for a place whose name comes from the depths of ancient myth.

There is a very old folk tale about the origin of Lough Foyle, one of the nine lakes that burst over land, which claims that its name means 'the borrowed lough'.

Two sisters dwelling beyond the Shannon, skilled in necromancy, made a deal, the one with the other. This story says that one of them was a hag who had a black heart. She asked her younger sister from Connemara (the wilderness on the western edge of Ireland) for the loan of a lake: 'Give me the loan of your silver lake, for I have none, and I promise to return it to you when tomorrow comes.' The Connemara witch rolled the lake up and sent it to her sister, only for her deceitful elder sister to then refuse to give it back: 'Ha, ye foolish child, what I meant to say from these lips of mine was – Judgement Day. I will keep your lake until the ending of time; for tomorrow, my sister, never ever comes.'

The River Foyle has shaped many of our lives, us border dwellers, and it is shaping them still. With Brexit, the river will shape-shift once more, to become a customs post: a threshold that must be crossed to pass from one place to the other, the ghost line made as visible as possible through human form. Already, on both sides of the border, police forces have stated they will not man any hard border that would be imposed once more on this island. The future of the Foyle, no matter who does or does not 'own' it, is back to being the stuff of near myth.

The year my father was born, 1963, grown men and young weans alongside one another, from both sides of the water in the city of Derry-Londonderry, played football matches on top of a frozen River Foyle. For many of these individuals, that winter of 'The Big Freeze' would be the first and last time they would ever 'set foot' on the other side of their fiercely divided city. Catholic lads on the left wing went well beyond the midway point on the ice; Protestant goalies pushed right up to within inches of the quay, far away from the safety of the Waterside where they belonged; each and every one of them was a foreigner in that alien, temporary and utterly neutral zone within their home town. All historical and imagined boundaries the river normally created were now displaced, dislocated, hidden from all view.

•

Just over a year ago, in November 2018, as that old year made moves to give up its delicate ghosts, I lay in Leeds and let a stranger draw a wild canary onto my left arm. There are many ways to handle shadows, and placing black ink on your body's surface is one of them. From the moment the bird made its way onto my skin, I haven't drunk a single drop of alcohol.

I had known for quite some years that alcohol was numbing me, keeping dark parts of me covered up with a thin film. I knew all those murky memories were still there, untouched, but they were being held safely far enough from my reach not to have to ever deal with them. Just like the childhood possessions people keep in their parents' loft years after moving away from home, I didn't need to worry about the chaotic pile of memories buried deep in that brain-bog-attic. Nor did I need to worry about the Beatrix Potter books, my first diaries, Missy (my Cabbage Patch doll) or the Sylvanian families I had loved so dearly. They were all left behind, long ago, one September, when our home in the predominantly Protestant Waterside council estate was petrol-bombed by sectarian youths, a handful of months after my father (the only Protestant who'd lived in the house) had left it. Derry-Doire-Londonderry in the 1990s is a place I have only just started to remember free from black smoke and bombs.

It is very recently indeed that I began to remember its disco with spangled bracelets and troll T-shirts the night after the president of America talked to us about bridges of peace. That city with its soldiers at the bus stop, at school, on the corner, at the border, the beach. With its helicopters keeping you from sleep, its surnames keeping you from everywhere that you wanted to go, its poverty keeping you either from, or in, trouble. With its barriers keeping you from everywhere, its boundaries keeping its everything away from its everything else.

I had never really 'been a drinker' as they say where I come from. I never went 'up the walls' as a teenager – with a tell-tale blue plastic or brown paper bag full of cheap alcohol. I never tried – the way many of my friends did – to carry myself *out* of myself – away elsewhere – with drink. I spent my teenage years, and all of my early twenties too scared of alcohol to even consider drinking a single drop. Alcohol had, and continues to have, an extremely destructive impact on members of both sides of my family. But at some dark point it caught up with me. Alcohol has been the only thing that has broken close relationships within the blood line that flows on each side of my lineage. It took me seven years to realise I was coursing along a track laid out for me decades earlier, by family members I loved but that I desperately didn't want to end up like.

Drink – and all the violence and sorrow it carries in its wake – terrified me. The night I first drank more than a sip – when I look back on it now – was the night I first began to feel the darkness from my past trickle out of me again, like melting ice under an unforgiving winter sun. I was twenty-eight, and just about to graduate from my Waldorf teacher training degree. I'd spent three years with a group of really wonderful, inspiring people but the whole time I'd felt an increasingly severe self-loathing and doubt. I was convinced that I would never, ever, be able to let go of all the baggage I was carrying around with me no matter how hard I tried. I never felt good enough, for anything or for anyone. I look back at that version of me and I so desperately want to reassure her with the experiences of almost a decade. Hindsight is an odd thing.

It was my birthday party, in the flat on the Meadows in

Edinburgh which I shared with three other women around my age. That year, as I moved towards the end of my first decade of adult life, things from my past were rearing their ugly, scary heads much more frequently than they had previously. Those memories, anxieties and heartaches seemed to have not only intensified but to come with much less warning than they had before. At the start they came in the form of mild panic attacks: difficulty breathing, lightheadedness and fear of crowded rooms. This was more or less manageable for a while; focusing on breathing helped, and taking off my shoes; it became a kind of surreal party trick in places, and with people I felt uncomfortable around. When it came to any form of long-term planning – trying to envisage where I might be in a year, or what I might be doing – it rattled me so much that I had to stop. I missed out on trips, didn't apply for courses, decided against going for promotions. I had begun to think about life as a place – like all those I'd live in – that I might be better off leaving. I was terrified to let people down but I knew I was close to a tipping point, and I had no idea what it would look like when the towers I'd built around myself could hold up no longer.

It made no sense back then. I'd moved so far away from where the trauma had all happened, and was leading a life that seemed successful – that looked so good on the surface. I had a secure job, a warm flat, good people to share it with, kind friends that accepted the coldness that often defined me. I was someone who had been let down so badly by those who were meant to look after me that I struggled with trust every step of the way. I had been looking out for myself, almost entirely, since my mid teens, and as a result of that I had no understanding of how to ask for help. This came across at many points, to many good people around me, as frosty and unfeeling – like I didn't need them, like I didn't need anyone or anything. I had lived a life with so few people in it, one where people and places came and went more quickly than the seasons, and I had no idea how to change that pattern, how to learn the way to allow people to stay.

I went back every few months to see my mum and younger brothers in Derry, and I constantly felt out of kilter. I had left Derry behind but I hadn't properly settled in Edinburgh either. I didn't fit in anywhere, and I didn't have people in either place that I felt I could talk to about what I was going through. I knew my mum had enough of her own stuff to carry and the friends I'd made in Edinburgh knew so little of what I'd gone through that I was at a complete loss to know where to begin.

If you fill a bucket of water so close to the brim that you can't really manage to carry it properly, the water will spill out at some point. You might lose the water in drips and drops – sloshing over the edges here and there – or you might lose the whole lot in one go, falling over with the weight that you could never have hoped to carry alone.

That first night I got drunk, nearing the end of my twenties, was my spilling point. The physical manifestation of the changes that had been happening deep inside me for a long time. In many spiritual circles, the year you turn twenty-eight is viewed as a massive turning point and marks a huge shift in your sense of self, and how you relate to that self, and to the experiences that self has gone through. It is called your 'Saturn return year', and is the point in your journey round the sun in which Saturn is in exactly the same position it was when you were born. The lead-up to this age starts in your late twenties and, many believe, the ripples of the transformation you experience might continue right through into your early thirties.

Whether you believe in the effects of the heavenly bodies or not, very often people seem to experience a deeply unsettling, utterly transformational period of their lives during these particular years. Past traumas often resurface, and there seems no way through without a crutch of one form or another. Everyone close to me was getting engaged, married, having children, buying cars and houses, travelling the world. I see now that for some of those people, these things were their buttress, the support that kept them upright in a life charged by changing winds. I, on the other hand, drank, and tried to pretend that I needed nothing and no one to deal with the past. I had buried it deep enough – I was sure – that I need not ever worry. I drank a little bit, almost every day. I very rarely socialised, and I very rarely got drunk. I mostly drank alone, a means of quietening things down inside my head, just enough to function. I drank in the way that meant that as soon as hard times came along, as they often did, I craved the numbness that a drink gave me more than I craved the taste of the drink itself. I drank as a way to drown out thoughts and memories that, if allowed to surface properly, I was sure would kill me, stone-cold and ghost-riddled.

I spent years trying over and over and over again to stop drinking. I bargained with myself; I played my self off against its own shadow-self. I knew then – as I still know now – that I drank as a form of self-harm. Self-hatred is an incredibly difficult thing to understand or to try to stop. Even trying to accept that I was abusing myself – over and over – was more difficult than I can really find the words for. I sometimes still feel like maybe I have no right to talk about these things – these feelings – these experiences that are fully mine to own, and to work through as best I can.

Then, on a fairly nondescript day in autumn 2018 – as a wedge of swans flew above me and below a whispered crescent moon – standing not in any sacred or special place but in a Derry laneway cluttered with a broken pram and black bin bags, I decided that before the new year came, I was going to stop. I decided that I was going to stop, and that I would do every single thing within my power to never ever start again. I knew the time had come to really face the experiences of my past face on – without the numbing help of a drink at the end of every single day. My past had been broken into pieces again and again due to alcohol, and I had no control over any of that. I thought I had got away untouched, unaffected, but I know now I was on exactly that same path of self-destruction and dependency as more people close to me than I care to even count. The time had come to let it all come to the surface. The time had come to allow it all to come back up from the place in which I'd tried to hide it. I was sick and tired of acting, of putting on a fake smile; I was tired of pretending I hadn't lived the life I had. I wanted to look at the things I had gone through. I wanted to hold them close, to give them the room they needed – to give *me* the room I needed – to heal.

•

I was completely and utterly unprepared for the nightmares that would come in the weeks that followed cutting alcohol out of my life. It felt as though they were coming out of every pore of my body. It felt as though they were poison that had been lying in wait for a very long time indeed, accumulating over the years. Even when we think we do not have a problem with something – that we could cope easily without it – the way our body responds when starved of the thing leaves us knowing that the body begs to differ. Detox nightmares, in my experience, make for warped and hideous viewing.

*I am in the front garden of our old house in the Waterside.*

The house is on fire but instead of flames licking the walls and steaming up the windows it is a monstrous cat with the body of a teenage boy – one of the three who, in real life, set fire to our home with a handmade petrol bomb when I was eleven.

*The house is multiple storeys high – and growing higher still.*

But the house has now become every single house my mum, dad and I have ever lived in, together or separately. The windows are locked and the keys I hold in my sweating hands are the keys for my brother's adulthood homes. I call to them all – my broken-up family – from an attic room, just as I am being wrapped up tightly inside a flag my granny crocheted out of her mother-in-law's scorched hair.

*My father watches the house he once shared with us, silently.*

My father is standing outside watching a black crow talk to the boys who are making the bomb, as though the crow is his apprentice or replacement. As if, when my dad left us on our own on that concrete battlefield, that heathen, feathered vagrant of a bird took his place at the table.

The reality of the night my family home was almost burned to the ground was, in actual fact, not that dissimilar to the nightmares in many respects. I was in my first year at big school. My wee brother was still in wee school. My mum was working three jobs just to scrape us all by after my dad left. A cat had, all out of nowhere, turned up the week before, and she refused to leave. She was black, and my brother and I knew in our bellies that she was magic.

When the bomb came, it was noiseless, but she heard it.

When the smoke came it was without a smell, but she smelled it.

The claw marks the cat left on my face when she was wakening me in my smoke-filled bedroom left me embarrassed in school for months, but she made sure I woke up. She made sure we all did. That magical creature.

My mother tried to stick it out, desperate to challenge the sectarianism that spilled out of all the cracks in the surfaces of our town. She wanted us to stay put, not to be put out. But as the days passed she accepted that the barrier had been built around us, and if we waited any longer we might not make it out at all.

We were not Protestant, now that Dad had left. We were not Catholic, either, though; our mum had lost the right to that – in the eyes of many – after marrying a Protestant. The fact that they had divorced made the situation so much worse, in the view of those who sought to keep the divisions in Derry alive and strong. We were nothing other than *other* – indefinable, unnamable, fallen down into the gaps in between. The truth is, we had *never* been either of these things – Protestant or Catholic – and to live in Derry in the '90s and to have neither of these words to fall back on left you in a harrowing hole of a place.

The new family that got allocated our home that week, after the bomb drove us out, threw every single thing we'd left behind into the back garden as soon as they moved in. When we went to look for our things – our photos and letters, our toys and baby hair in envelopes, our yellow teapot, our mum's beauty pageant trophies, our things found during walks on Donegal beaches across the hard border, we watched the equally hard new family pretend we weren't there. There were no curtains for them to draw to keep our eyes away from looking into the house we had called home. It made no difference anyway, as no person or item could be properly made out through the (already bogging dirty) windows of the smoke-scorched house.

We watched unidentifiable forms become wraith-like. The

forms moved in the half-dark. They took off from a sofa we couldn't see but we knew was the black leather sofa that we had left behind: ghost vultures.

The childhood belongings were easy, so easy in fact, to forget. The human-size silken crow I met in my smoke-filled, fear-thick bedroom was not so easy to shake out of my head, unsurprisingly.

He came that night, as if from a nightmare I couldn't waken up from, and he was as real to me as the scratches that were left on my cheek.

He didn't creaaak or crawww.

He didn't fly or peck at the floor.

He didn't search for food, or for dead things.

He did not lick the blood from my wounds.

He forcibly ignored the cat that was keening at us both.

When the smoke was at its thickest and most choking, he remained stone-cold silent, and as still as something long, long dead.

The cheap door in the room had warped in the heat of the fire and it wouldn't let me open it. The door would not let me leave. Somehow, the coal-black crow managed to land on the door. I watched as the wood lost its whiteness, as it gave itself over into the hands of a murderous, taunting bird. A bird that painted it black.

That September night in 1995 – the year the Peace Process began, the first time I met my crow – he laughed and laughed and laughed at me but no sound escaped out of his smooth black beak. He laughed until I somehow found the strength to ram the door open into the hallway. Strength that I knew back then was definitely not mine. Strength that I knew he had categorically not expected me to find.

I made it out from that blackened room. The cat did too. All of us made it out from the burning house . . . in a physical way, anyhow. The crow was waiting for us all on that middle-of-the-night street.

I was the only one who could see him. The only time I ever made him disappear was when I drank. It did not make him silent, though; alcohol never took away his voice. I am the only one who has ever heard it. I could pick out his tone from a murder of millions.

He has come into every bedroom in every house I have moved to since.

There is untold darkness to the world that we have been given, and after many years of battling against that darkness I have learned to be still in its presence. To lay a place for it at the table, to sit with its black feather-tips, to let its echoes dance across the landscape of my insides when the sadness comes, silent like a fox.

•

When I was nine and my wee brother was seven he carried a water rat home inside a Teenage Mutant Ninja Turtles bumbag. He had been playing at the stream beside our house when his plastic killer whale from London Zoo was carried away by careless water rushing over slimy stones. The sun had started to creep behind old trees and new council houses, and his friends made their way home with grubby hands and freckling faces. But he didn't join them up the concrete steps back to our house.

Teatime came and the smell of stew filled our yellow kitchen. I laid three bowls on our wooden table, trying to cover up the bit where we'd carved our initials using the spare back-door key. When he still hadn't come back, Mum went to 'do the rounds'. He could have been with the Gillespie boys playing Nintendo, 'fishing' with wee Craig, or climbing the big ivy wall behind Tommy's shop. He'd be safe, anyway – because that's how things were back then on our housing estate – togetherness in the face of hardship. Way back then, before the activities of our Protestant council estate reached their lowest point, folk were good to each other. They looked out for each other. There was more that kept us together back then than the things that later crept in to cleave us apart.

When she returned, an hour later – sheet-white and shaken – she found us stroking a beautiful, warm water rat in the downstairs toilet. Three Fridays later, at dusk, a mangled, close-to-dying urban fox followed us from the top of the housing estate, where the main road grew out of the scrub boundary of the football field, right onto our back doorstep. I wonder, these days, if those creatures could smell the loss of our father off our young, mucky skin. I wonder if they could see what was held in store for us, just a wee bit in the future. I wonder if that cat could see it, too. I still remember how calm the rat was that night, as my brother held it delicately in his little boy hands.

·

The coal-black crow that came into my path that September night has yet to leave my side. Some days he is like the midnight ebony edges around a blue moon, soft and carrying only a whisper of violence in his beak. But some days he is huge and folkloric, carrying unthinkable grief on the tips of his wings as he crouches over me, hiding the light away like an eclipse.

The echoes of the Troubles in Ireland have been, are being and will continue to be a coal-black crow that covers us with its wings. In those moments between waking and sleeping, while the border between reality and nightmare dances, the past, if it has not been dealt with, will keep resurfacing. It is my belief, though, that we are learning to talk to that crow, these days. We are learning to talk with each other, too. How do we talk about things which are so real they are almost unbelievable? I spent decades trying to accept my own story, trying to make peace with the sorrow and the unending, haunting grief.

The smell of young flesh beginning to burn, just singed enough to register in the brain. The way a cheap door warps – as a pink room fills with thick black smoke – and the ripples in the wood look like the sea, like the sea on a violent, volatile night. The way that a smooth face bleeds in a way so different from a weathered, split knee. How a mangy stray cat, when called upon for action, can be as loyal as any dog. How, when your house has been set alight, you really *do* abandon everything – arrow-swift, nightmare-shook, carrying less than nothing in your blackening hands.

How do we talk about these things?

Ebony-black feathers, glistening at the end of a little-girl bed like oil spilled on a wet road? A man-sized crow that arrived on the day the world changed shape, and never really went away, no matter how many times you told him he wasn't real.

The experiences I had in that childhood home, in the Waterside of Derry, less than a mile from where I now live, burrowed down deep, like a cough that has settled. They left their shards here and there, underneath the surface and right down into the bone and the marrow.

There are places that are both hollowed and hallowed all in one. They have wounded us, but we must return to them if we want to try to loose their tight hold on us. The places watch as we lose our way, as we are sent away, as we run away; they wait in stillness for us to find our way back.

## CHAPTER FOUR

## *Snow Light*

THE WINTER OF THE YEAR I started secondary school, the snow came to Derry, blown in from Russia, but another important visitor arrived just before the snow. Bill Clinton – then President of the United States of America – addressed the biggest crowd I have ever seen in Derry's Guildhall Square. I didn't know anything about him at all, except that that morning my mum and her best friend had served him his breakfast in the hotel where they both worked. He stood tall in front of the bright Christmas lights, and as soon as he began to talk I could feel something inside me shift and change shape. He spoke of peace, in language I had never heard before. He talked about divisions between people, and about the difference between people who want to make peace and those who want to prevent it, who want to remain caught up in the terrifying chaos of our 'normal' lives in the North of Ireland.

As a child of a mixed-religion family which had only just been broken up – largely due to the violence in our bombed-out, bruised and broken city – listening to the conviction in that man's voice as he beckoned all of us in front of him on a journey towards a future built on peace, I knew that something had changed in me. I wasn't even a teenager yet but I knew that I wanted things to be different – *so* different – from how they were.

A metamorphosis began as I stood there shivering in the freezing Derry air. Clinton ended his speech by quoting Seamus Heaney. This was the first time I had ever heard the great poet's words, and the ones the president chose that day are still the words that I have been most moved by in all my life:

> *So hope for a great sea-change*
> *On the far side of revenge.*
> *Believe that a further shore*
> *Is reachable from here.*

More than two decades have passed since Clinton's speech, and Ireland has experienced such deep-rooted change in the years between. Voices, once silenced, now echo loudly. Since the Brexit vote, the Irish border has been on more people's minds than ever imagined possible before.

I lived away from my island for most of my adult years – witnessing its transition from a place far away – my view foggy and obscure. I have been 'home' for three years now and I finally feel that I can see past the fog. I spent lots of time exploring the lands of Scotland, Wales and England in my twenties, places that have changed me and allowed the process of healing to begin. But my draw to place, into the wild and unknown parts of the landscape around me, the pull that dragged me in close, started here in Ireland. It started in the North, right here where the border of the island weaves its path.

Derry was a dark city to be in and I was scared. My baby brother was scared. Our mum must have been terrified, although we didn't know it back then. During the worst moments, we were taken across the border – away from all that was burning and bleeding around us – into the heart of rural Donegal. We would be collected straight from school, in a car we could not afford to tax or insure, and cross a hard border manned by British soldiers. I see us both so clearly in the backseat, crouched down. The only way we could tell that Mum was scared was because she didn't turn the radio back on after we made it across the border; we couldn't see her shaky hands, or into her tired single-mum face from our in-between space behind her.

That temperamental red Volvo allowed our mum to take her children as far away as she could with whatever spare fuel money she had from working long, hard shifts in the hotel. She took us from beach to cove, over bog-land to woods, alongside streams into fields – allowing the invisible line of the border to act as some unseen, mythical protector. We were delivered across it through grace that felt sent from a place unknown – fabled, and with an urgent sense of secrecy. Many of the places we spent time in, I realised later, were places where the veil was gossamer thin, if it was even there at all. We spent days upon days in places bathed in deep and indefinable energy. We walked in two worlds, in a way – woven together, knitted so loosely, with such delicacy, that separation faded, even if only for a moment.

Childhood is already a place with its own energy and reckoning; memories and their recollection are, too. We remember the exact same thing so differently from one another; the past is a place of metamorphosis, a dance between us and things unseen, ever shifting. When we try to piece all the parts back together to make the whole, we are left slipping through the wet, changing sands. Like memory, and like childhood, thin places are experienced by each of us in entirely different ways. You bring your own self to the table, and your relationship to that self; place is there to hold us and to let the echo bounce back in those exquisite, ethereal encounters. Certainly they have the potential to exist everywhere, in every country, but the power of place is felt very strongly in Ireland and Britain, and the places people most commonly describe as feeling thin are sacred and spiritual sites such as stone circles, cashels, burial sites, holy wells, blessed rivers and ancient ruins. Many of the places in which I have felt a sense of quiet, otherworldly awe have been such places as these.

In my thirties I have done much looking back; I have allowed memories to flood over me like a winter sunrise. And I have been reminded, over and over, of places where no stones lie, no bodies are held, no bones are sealed, no water is revered – soft, elusive places, found in the least likely of locations. One of the thinnest places I have ever been was at the periphery of a field, at the top of a laneway, looking down onto a rough, sectarian housing estate – the second of my childhood – on the edges of Derry.

Long before I was born, every single street on our new housing estate had at least one cherry blossom tree planted at the end of it. We had been staying with some friends after the petrol bomb, and one day – just after school – Mum and my stepdad went out to view the new house the council had offered us. They arrived back at teatime, as the early autumn light was streaming into the front room, peach-pale and shimmering. One of the first things my mum said was that there were cherry blossom trees. The only thing we had had in the small front garden of our last house – the one we were bombed out of – was a cherry blossom tree. There wasn't really any need for our mum to say anything more. We definitely couldn't keep sleeping on the floor of her colleague's house, which had already been too full before we'd all shown up in the dead of one September night, coughing like sailors and shaken through, ghosts of ourselves.

We moved into the new house in the same month as we'd moved out of the old one. We moved in, at first, with only the clothes we stood in and the handful of things we'd been able to rescue from the old house. We had nothing at all, at the beginning, except the bare essentials.

This new house was on the other side of the River Foyle, on an equally sectarian housing estate, except this one was a Catholic housing estate. As soon as anything sectarian happened to a family or individual, they were moved into a similar type of house, but in the opposite type of area. I suppose it was the only thing the people working in the Housing Executive Office could think to do really, to try to make sure it didn't happen again. It's still what they do, even now. Areas in Derry that are supposed to be 'mixed' still often have a way of finding their chosen side. This new estate was very similar to the last one, as housing estates often seem to be. Small patches of green dotted around – not enough to play or plant on – communal concrete squares, too many humans in one small area, the insistent squealing of electricity meters running on empty.

The thing which made this one stand out from the last one was the fact that this estate was built on the hill Amelia Earhart had crashed her plane into, in May 1932. Our new house was at the very top of that hill – right where the new estate ended and gave the land back to itself – overlooking the River Foyle and the fated city it flows through. I think back so often now on the many different views I had of that river – at all her stages, with all her bridges and mouths, all her thin, hidden places. Every house I lived in was within sight of the River Foyle, even though I lived on opposite sides of it, and eventually moved miles outside of Derry, right where the river becomes a salty, reed-fringed estuary. A body of water knows no definite form, no true boundaries, no borders. She is held delicately in the in-between place, carrying us in her strong flow to spaces unknown, unmapped territories.

When Amelia Earhart began to ready herself to crash-land in a place she had never before set eyes on, above green hills and sprawling farmland, one of the last things she would have seen in the underworld beneath her plane was that meandering

77

River Foyle. Blue and steady, hungry and steeped in myth. She would, most likely, have known very little about the city where she was about to land. The border she had flown above had been in place for just over a decade. From her bird's-eye view, she would have been completely unaware of there even *being* a border at any point in that unmarked world below her. She would have been unaware of there being lines on the surface of the landscape – veins through which a thing not dissimilar to blood could be channelled, leaving no trace. Of there being invisible cracks beneath the surface that broke the land up and spat it back out. Amelia Earhart could not see the debris that already littered that wild and ancient city of oaks – shrapnel that was so small it seemed it could never really be taken out from under the skin. Amelia Earhart could not see the broken parts of the city and its people – nor the sorrow and trauma that would eventually leak into the belly of the land – lying quietly below her.

The border that Earhart had flown across at least once before she crash-landed in a field in Derry-Doire-Londonderry was utterly invisible. If she were able somehow to return to that same field now, a century later, she would still see no sign whatsoever of any physical boundary below her feet. Her eyes – sharp and inquisitive though they were – would search and search for the markers between the North and the South, between there and here, to no avail. There is no trace of a dividing line in those fields to which we moved after being petrol bombed out of our home on the opposite bank of the River Foyle. That border – the one that has been being debated and contested for the entirety of the Brexit debate of the last years – the one that lives have been lost over, is a thing Amelia Earhart could never have held in her eager explorer hands. No matter how hard any of us may try to grasp at it – to define its outline and draw its skeleton, to mark its place on the land's skin like a shadow stitched on with rope – it slips away from us like the first butterfly of the summer, too otherworldly to feel real and not dissimilar, I realise now, to any thin place on earth.

That Christmas *sneachta* – the snow – came to Earhart Park. It was the only Christmas we would spend there on the city-side of the River Foyle; we stayed for less than a year. We were just as unwelcome on both sides of that river, and were bullied out before we'd even properly unpacked. It was the only Christmas Day of my life until then that had ever brought snow. It still is.

The fields beyond the top lane led us, without any marker, to the place where Derry became Donegal, and the idea of places shape-shifting became a central and haunting one for me that winter. The lessons that winter carried in its icy breath have stayed with me for my whole life. There is something, too, about snow that weaves reality in alongside something else. The land is not the same land it was before the snow fell, somehow. It casts a spell – rather, we cast some kind of spell – over the day. There is a sense of something unknown, a sense of white-cloaked wonder. I looked up the word *sneachta* recently, and the dictionary listed three ways to use it in a sentence: '*driven snow*', '*the snows of yester-year*', but – most intriguingly for me – was the final entry: '*nothing would surprise me more*'. The Irish language itself has imbued snow with something that comes at you all out of nowhere, something which creeps up behind you and takes the wind right out of your sails. We cannot really know what is held within snow's ethereal whiteness. What was once there before may now be gone. Where lines once were, now there might only be an eternal void of nothingness.

This new housing estate was surrounded by Irish Traveller stopping grounds. There were horses roaming the fields. Huge fires were lit in their fields most evenings, and they were so different from the fires the other folk we lived alongside lit. The fires the Travellers lit were for warmth, not destruction like the sectarian bonfires that were built like wooden towers on both sides of the river. The Travellers' fires were for gathering around and for something else I couldn't quite name back then. I think I understand their fires a little better now.

I encountered, for the first time that winter, folk that refused to be easily named or kept in one place – living here and there, always on the move, only ever found temporarily in those liminal, unmapped places. I met – accidentally, awkwardly – people who, like us, were a wee bit *unwanted* in the places where they had turned up. A wee bit too different from the people over on the estate to be ever fully welcomed. But the thing that intrigued me most of all was the fact that those people were more than fine when the time came for them to move along. In fact, maybe they even craved it. Their roots, it seemed, were long enough to make *any* place feel like home, no matter how stony the ground.

On 21 May 1932, Amelia Earhart made aviation history as the first woman to fly solo across the Atlantic, landing just outside Derry in a city-side area known as Cornshell. More specifically, she landed in Gallagher's field. More specifically – even still – she landed in the field above our new house. When asked later why she had done it, what it was that had driven her to make that journey, what had emboldened her for such a courageous undertaking, she replied: *'I just wanted to see if I could fly the Atlantic alone. We all fly Atlantics in our own way . . .'*

The history of flight is the history of a dream. It speaks of courage and of diving into the unknown: places outwith our everyday maps. What is it about being suspended above the earth that holds such intrigue for us? Flight is one of the most common dreams people have at key moments in their lives. We are, when we fly, neither on solid ground nor in the open air. It is a place all of its own making.

Humans have dreamed of flight for moons upon moons, perhaps since dreaming began. We imitate birds. We try to mirror their ways – to be winged and full of untethered freedom; we try to fly. The humans in our legends and fairytales, our folklore and myth, are often able to fly and we have grown up with the desire for wings embedded in our being. Ancient Chinese, Persian, Roman, Arabic and Celtic people have all tried to fly. Monks, scholars, warriors and craftsmen tried to build flying machines. We are a race that longs to be a winged one. One of the earliest and best-known accounts of flight comes from Greek mythology. Daedalus angered King Minos – ruler of the island of Crete – and had to flee immediately.

The inventor Daedalus collected enough feathers from the eagles that flew above him to make wings. Minos' men were within firing distance now. He took his son to the edge of the cliff, placed wings on their human forms, and made for the sky's uncharted territory. Daedalus instructed his son to fly in the middle – to hold his place in the in-between, to have the courage to be neither here nor there. The end of the story is well known to many. Icarus, intoxicated with the thrill of flying, flew too high. The wax melted on his wings, and the feathers fell out. He was left flapping his bare arms. Daedalus watched his son fall into the depths of the waters below, swallowed up whole by the belly of the sea.

We weren't exactly living on a cliff by the edge of the sea that winter when I turned twelve, but we were closer to water than we had been before, and its presence was a constant source of nourishment. We were – despite being surrounded by concrete and the leftover spoilage of constant rioting – located merely a handful of miles from the wetlands of Inch Island and from the vast mouth of the River Foyle. In the midst of police vans being burned right through to their metal innards, destruction and horrific violence (instigated by weans so young they should have already been asleep), swans and geese flew over our heads, calling in the hazy sky above us all. Almost every single time I saw these beautiful, majestic birds, I understood deep to my core what had spurred Amelia Earhart on. What could be more life-changing, more light-filled, than to look down at this broken, circling and gorgeous world from the same place as the birds we share it with?

Those days on that city hill, on the edges of so many things, were filled, no matter what new struggles came, with the wild world in all its living wonder. Violence had become the norm for thousands of us, but I knew – even then – that it was far from 'normal'. Witnessing violence of the kind we did – so often, so intimately, to such a destructive end – does something to you. You are changed for ever. Life as you know it continues, day in, day out: as unending as time, and as constant as the falling rain. You try to slot in, to fit in the same lines that had been drawn for you, but you feel too hefty now; you have too much weight around your neck.

You listen to swans that you don't know then are called whooper swans. You wonder why they keep coming back to land at all. Why would they ever choose to land in your part of the world? You watch murmurations of starlings on yet another night of rioting, and you want to know what the birds know. What draws them towards one another in dance. What keeps them so close together and what taught them how to gather, how to be so delicate with one another.

You go into school. You sit with people who only see violent things – those things like bonfires and scorched skin, flags and kneecappings – on the news. Whose parents warn them not to be friends with weans who live on housing estates. You do your Latin test all about the importance of thresholds in Ancient Roman literature, squeezing your eyes shut so tightly that it gives you a headache. You squeeze them shut to try to forget about the things *you* have seen at thresholds. The things that have come to *your* door in the last few months. You squeeze your eyes shut until the bell rings and then you go back outside into the world, to look for swans.

•

The ending of our time at Earhart Park came as swiftly as night falls, as swiftly as winter seems to come upon us all. The events of the ending all happened so quickly – exactly as they had in the old house. One Sunday afternoon I was at home with my stepdad on our front doorstep, listening to the lads across the square talking about Celtic football team, just as the youth club leader at my granny's (Protestant) church turned up to collect me. Emblazoned all over the minibus were the signs that gave away the fact that we weren't like the rest of the people living on that street. The words that gave us away as being different, in fact, from every other person on that estate, different from almost every other person who lived on the city-side of the River Foyle. The bus was covered in blue writing: *Clooney Hall Methodist Church Londonderry*. This was the sign that said that we were – in the words of the lad in the house opposite from us – '*dirty orange bastards that needed put the fuck out*'.

Things quickly went from bad to worse: rumours spread through the estate like wildfire, and very soon enough of the right people had made it clear that we would be taking a huge risk to stay. We didn't wait to be 'put out' this time. We couldn't call on the friends we had stayed with last time – we were on their side of the water now – these were 'their

84

people' who wanted us gone, and you just didn't argue back then; you still don't, even now.

I am not sure if my mum and her partner would even have really discussed the options. There were none, so that made it a wee bit easier, I suppose. There was nothing that the housing association could do. They had no real options either. Where were they meant to place us? We were neither Protestant nor Catholic, and our parents had stayed together in a mixed marriage long enough to ensure that none of the essential parts of either of these camps could ever be instilled in us. At least not to the extent that we could claim either heritage. My brother didn't want to leave his Protestant school in the Waterside, close to where we had been petrol bombed. He knew, even at such a young age, that he had no hope of learning the new language he would have needed to get by in a new school, a Catholic one, on the city side. The other weans could smell a traitor, it seemed. They would try to catch us out, every chance they got, and they always succeeded. When they asked about our Holy Communions, our confessions and our da, we hadn't a hope in hell – either the Catholic or Protestant one. We didn't fit in in the city side as fully as we hadn't fitted in in the Waterside. We weren't quick enough to learn that new language and had nothing to fall back on. We didn't know what the answer was for which football team we supported; we had never even heard of Gaelic football, and none of the surnames we were able to switch between served us any favours. We were caught completely and utterly in the gaps between those two firmly rooted identities. That space in the middle was a terrifying and isolating place, and none of us ever really could have felt safe at any point along the way.

The threat of serious violence crept back into our lives again. So we ran, again, in the night, with what we could carry, on the dawn of St Patrick's Day. The snow had been gone for two months, and spring was working away silently at making the land new again. The cherry blossom had started to come out and the trees on the laneway were full of goldfinches. I realised, without even thinking about it, that I was going to miss them, and wondered if there would be trees at our next house.

•

It is a November afternoon more than two decades since that winter spent at the top of a hill, two fields away from the border. There is a single sparrow on the roof of the house two doors up from mine. There is a howling wind – the weather this year has been unsettled, squally, as though it is making to speak for the world – and the potted trees in the yard have fallen over onto the blue hydrangea. They are young oaks, only just turned three. I bought them the summer I moved back to Derry, right as the Brexit chaos we are now witnessing was first born. Those trees – emblems of my once-divided city – are reminders of so much. Of hope, of resilience, of unbreakable roots – where we come from, what we live through, what our future holds. I have found it increasingly difficult to look at those young trees, this year. There are other things nestled in alongside the hope they once represented; their growth speaks of unwelcome and terrifying change. Change that most of Northern Ireland, most of the UK, most of Europe seem vastly unprepared for.

I think of roots, and I think of belonging, of kinship and community. I think of that community beneath our feet, and of all that their knitted ways could teach us. Trees talk to one another, always. No tree is left alone and, in times of need, the goodness held inside the other trees – no matter how far away they may be from the sick one – is shared with the tree that is suffering. I think of trauma – those inflicted and those we inflict. I want to trust that we are going to learn from this mess – a mess we did not ask for, and which seems to be getting worse as the year marches on.

The sparrow seems as though it does not notice the storm that is gathering itself up in the thick and keen air. Its nest must be in the eaves, and it cheeps – one small and deep call after the other – unstoppably, full of resolute dedication.

I have been affected by patterns for as long as I can remember. By the order and sequence of things and events, by the symbolism that can be strung together for our lives from small, quiet, delicate artifacts. Items that we find, or that find us, that meld together and form skeins of meaning in an otherwise confusing, murky sky. I have been bringing found things into my spaces for decades, since the week my father left home. I have found such soothing nourishment in stone and wood, shell and bone – in solitary feathers and fallen things, in skeletal seed-heads, and in things no longer living. I cherish these gifted objects, and the very act of finding them, laying value on the precise moment of my life in which these exquisite offerings entered in. I keep them close, and, at times when the day feels heavy as a steel grey sky, I lift the one I feel most drawn to, the one I need to carry with me on that given day.

Our ancestors found meaning in happenings and patterns. They sought to foresee the future in the way birds swirled above hills, the way light fell on a stone, the amount of days without rain – or snow – or death. Winged creatures in particular have long been used to unravel messages for the humans they share the earth with. Magpies, crows, owls, cuckoos and many more birds carry wisdom from the past that is hard to shake off in our collective memory. We have always looked up as well as down. Many years after I lived on the hill that she crashed into, I found the final words that Amelia Earhart spoke. During her final flight she become caught up in extreme difficulties, far away from home and far away from Earhart Park. Her last words were these: '*We are running north and south.*' Nothing further was ever heard from her.

The winter we spent at Earhart Park, geese and swans flew above me many times a day in a salmon-pink sky that smelled of the first coming of snow. I had never really noticed the way the sky behaved before. I had never before noted the way that colour can spill out over the edges of the sky – onto tin roofs, into the eyes of horses – how it can fill the whole world within your reach. I had never realised how light worked before that winter.

Light that is neither here nor there. Light that comes from nowhere at all, and from everywhere, too.

Light that feels like such a gift, a guide, a way to feel strong and safe. Light that will fall onto the land and the water no matter what is happening there, no matter what might have already happened there, no matter what may come to that body of water – that stretch of land – in the days ahead.

Light that must, like the birds, have been throwing itself down onto the patch of land you are standing on, dirtied underfoot with muddied snow, for many moons before you came along.

Light that will still shine down when the snow is gone, when you are gone, just as white and silent. Light that is as much an offering as anything you could bring into your space. Light that you cannot hold close in any physical, tangible way but that you see, decades later, that you have carried with you from brick building to brick building – across seas and borders, from place to place.

Light that holds you in place. Light that calls you with it, to any and every place it falls.

# CHAPTER FIVE

## *Lost Things*

WHEN LOSS COMES ONTO OUR path, the circles through which the moon travels fall all out of kilter. Time seems out to trick you, and everything feels foggy: grey and shrouded. The loss of one thing, I well know, can send a flare from a myriad of other times – other places – reminding us of anything and everything that we have already lost along the way, the fire of today burning kindling from a time long gone.

We were intimidated out of Earhart Park during the only spring we spent there. Our next move took us away from Derry entirely, to Ballykelly, a small village, where my then stepdad grew up. It was like a whole other world entirely, despite not even being twenty miles from the city.

It was quiet there, and calm, a kind of place I had never known before. Everyone knew each other, and friendships there seemed to be above any idea of difference. No one there cared what school I went to, what my background had been, or anything even remotely along those lines. When my stepdad's sister took me to meet some of her friends, people that in turn became my friends, the first question I was asked was what my favourite Nirvana song was. Further chats were about why I was a vegetarian, why I didn't smoke weed, and if I was scared of haunted houses. My stepdad was so loved there, and we were welcomed fully to the village as his family. Life felt bright, and much less scary. Years went by, peacefully, and nothing felt remotely like it had in Derry.

We were young, my group of friends, and we were a very close bunch of teenagers, made much closer by the sheer fact of boredom. Ours was a youth free from technology, in a sleepy village with two pubs, one pool table and a chip shop that we made and broke our young loves outside, with a half-bag of chips between us. It was the first time in my entire life that I hadn't been constantly watching over my shoulder, wondering if I was allowed to be where I was in the school uniform I wore, or with the background I had. We all came from both backgrounds – it was an entirely mixed village. Protestants and Catholics were neighbours in Ballykelly, and everything felt exactly as I had always imagined it should. We looked out for each other. We argued and we got jealous and we fixed it the very next day. Most of my friends who came from there – not blow-ins like me – were related to each other. I never once said it out loud to another person but for the first time since that crow turned up in my bombed-out bedroom, I felt something close to safe. I felt as if nothing could ever go wrong there, as if I could finally let everything from the past go.

There is a darkness to the world we have been given, though, and such unthinkable violence in the paths we create along the way. Before the night that my room was petrol-bombed, I had never known that there was a map inside of me. A pathway that would continue to be drawn and redrawn; another invisible borderline, beneath the surface. I hid my grief under my skin.

There had been so much loss I had lost count. Names, faces, houses, accounts, family members, toys, books, trees, wellies, words – all bled into one. What is the shared collective noun for such loss?

Even in Ballykelly, loss lingered at the edges. We had lived there five years when mum's partner began, all out of nowhere, to drink in a way I don't recall him having done before. I remember it as becoming something he did every single day, sometimes to the stage that he didn't know who he was, or where. He moved out of our house when I was sixteen, the first of two devastating losses that year held.

That year also saw the first death of a friend, something altogether different from every loss before it. He was eighteen; I was sixteen. He was my closest male friend, the only boy I'd slept beside in a bed, the first person to give me a Valentine's card. He had curtains in his hair, held in place with thick, gunky gel; his waves were as sculpted as Binevenagh Mountain, and as blond as a cherub. He was murdered, most likely less than an hour after I said goodbye to him. His bloodstained clothes were found the next day, as we all searched for him, terrified, within sight of my home – practically next door to his own.

The trail of events leading up to his death had all been

normal: nothing out of place, nothing to make anyone worry. The murder of a kind, funny, popular eighteen-year-old came as the biggest and deepest shock – not just to me, of course, but to the entire, small, close-knit village. For the first few hours of that Sunday morning, every one of us believed he would walk around the next corner. We all kept wondering whose house he had crashed at (he didn't like going home after having had a drink as his parents didn't approve) but all of us knew, though none of us wanted to be the one to say it, that he hadn't turned up at any of our houses that Saturday night. If he had been going to, it would have been mine, or his cousin's – our three houses made a triangle on the hill that led from Ballykelly to Glack, a hamlet a few miles away where some of our friends lived. We all kept saying how much he'd laugh (what a contagious, living laugh) when he caught us all out looking for him like on some dodgy crime series on TV. How he'd secretly be really upset with himself for putting us all through the worry – especially his wee mam. At the point where the silence came into the picture, when we stopped talking about what he would or wouldn't do when he walked around the corner, it all changed, and it never went back to how it had been before.

That night our friend had walked me up home from the village chip shop, and we chatted about life on the short, dark walk. He made me laugh, so very much; it took me years to find people that made me laugh the way he had. My mum was working nights back then, so I went to sleep, and he headed back down to join the rest of our friends – the ones who could easily sneak into the two local pubs, even if they weren't the right age. Afterwards, as normal, they would all stand outside the chippy for another wee while, messing with each other in the cold, finding joy in places that not everyone might think to look.

That next day, a Sunday at the end of April 1999, my gorgeous, kind, funny friend's clothes were found by a policeman – his cousin – in a wee clearing beside his house where we would all often hang out at night. My friend, that blond-haired, joyful, cheeky young man, the funniest person I had ever met, was found miles up the hill, in ancient woods.

Rather, his body was found. The bloodied, battered, utterly broken shell of a body that was found – in a shallow grave, in Loughermore Forest – was not my friend. My friend is still that beautiful person who treated us all as if we were worthy of deep joy, and laughter. I need for that abused body to be in no real way linked with my friend. I need to know that the only people for whom that body has any relevance are the people who put my gentle, calm friend through what they did, just fifteen hours before his body was unearthed. One person was charged back then, despite all of our village and the army camp inside it being interviewed and monitored for months upon months. The man who served time was a neighbour of my friend, of us all, and he was charged with disposing of the body. He never shared the details that we begged for, never admitted who murdered our friend, his neighbour. It broke our village apart. It took everything we thought was real life and turned it into a warped inversion of itself. I don't know if I will ever be able to find the words to describe the horror of that time. I have tried to, on almost every anniversary, and try as I may, it never feels real. The words are shadows of themselves; they make a ghost of a boy who was far, far from that. My closest female friend from that time – from that group – said this year that she remembers the darkness, that everything remained dark for quite some time. I don't remember that part; I guess I was maybe a bit more used to an absence of light. If I'm honest, which it has taken me such a long time to be, I remember knowing that my childhood had absolutely and definitely ended then. We never skinny-dipped again in the waterfall up the hill; we never dared each other to kiss behind the chapel on the way to Glack; we stopped walking the back lanes holding hands and talking about where we would all live (next door to one another on the two old estates on the Shore Road, beside the horses and the oaks); we all, every single one of us young ones, lost something we could never dream of clawing back.

In relation to what our friend's family had lost, our pain paled in comparison. But I see now, twenty years on, that our loss was still a vast one. Hardly any of us kept in touch. Many of us suffered depression; many of us still do. Some of us who said we'd stay, left, and it is looking like we may have left for ever. Some of us who wanted to leave – to live a life very different from that in a wee sleepy village – stayed, and married our next-door neighbour, and bought houses next door to our own parents. It broke something in us, that murder of one of the best people we knew. It broke something in me so huge that it has taken two decades to try to fix it, to forgive the world for taking such a beautiful thing and beating it back down into the soil. To forgive humanity for allowing the neighbour of someone I loved to carry his broken body in a car – up to an ancient forest that I loved – and to bury him, without ever explaining what happened, who did it, or why. It has taken me twenty years to try to accept that that same person apparently played golf a handful of hours later, as people he had grown up with, was related to, shared a life with, searched through fields, laneways and hidden places to find the body that he had buried. It has taken me twenty years to accept, and to let go of, the guilt that I felt when I used to think – for a fleeting moment – how I had already experienced enough loss before that Sunday. That I had been given too much from the pot, and I could take no more sorrow – especially not something that heavy, that unbearably black. I spent years trying to play it down; I was so terrified of making his murder about me. It wasn't about me – I wasn't his poor mamma, his lovely sister, his da or his wee brother, who was left to be his grieving mam's only son. I'd known my friend for far fewer years than our other friends, and we weren't related either.

Now I see that we may all experience the same loss, in a way, but our backgrounds, our home lives, our experiences, differ so greatly, that we will naturally all feel the ripples so differently, so individually. What I experienced when I lost my friend was so intrinsically linked with my own ideas about home, belonging and safety. How could it not be? I associated every single thing about Ballykelly, from then on, with the loss of him. It's what I had done with all of the places I'd already had to leave: making things black and white – good and bad, safe and dangerous – made it easier to cut all ties. Slowly I watched, as if from the sidelines, as I built a picture once more in my head and told myself it was okay to leave there, just as I'd left everywhere else. It was a place of unrivalled suffering, and nothing could ever turn it back into an almost safe place; nothing could bring back the sense of calm and belonging I had once felt there.

When my mum and her new partner sold the house that same year and moved to Edinburgh with his job, I did the thing I knew made it all easier to cope with. I walked away from Ballykelly, and every single thing it represented, and pretended I had never even set foot in the place. Nothing was the same after that year, the year we all entered the next millennium. Fear held me tightly in the belly of its storm, and my identity, which had once seemed so fiercely outlined as a teenager, had faded at the edge; the lines of my map had blurred and I didn't have a compass.

Grief is a country that has no definite borderlines and that recognises no single trajectory. It is a space that did not exist before your loss, and that will never disappear from your map, no matter how hard you rub at the charcoal lines. You are changed utterly, and your personal geography becomes yours and yours only.

•

When my friend died, I internalised lots of the trauma instead of processing it properly, likely because this was the norm for me; it was simply another layer added onto the pile. For months after he died I was repeatedly taken out of school and questioned by the police; most of us were. Instead of trying to process – at the tender age of sixteen – the loss of one of the kindest, gentlest people I have ever been loved by, I ran. I ran from the place he had inhabited with such brightness. For two full years, he came to me in my dreams as a white bird. Sometimes, but not always, an egret, like the ones we'd all watched together at the Shore Road – not always visible in the dream, either, always white though, always a white bird.

When the dreams stopped, a handful of years passed in various different houses on the island of Ireland – with my grandparents first, then in any room in any flat in Dublin for as long as I could afford the rent. I was living in a cramped, damp bedsit in the Northside of the city – a place where I'd had to board the window up with wood after a drug addict had broken the glass with an axe – when I was told I had been growing cells on the inside of me. I was told that I'd been growing them for a number of years, likely: cells that needed to be cut out. Cells on my cervix that needed cut out sharply, swiftly.

I've spent so much of this last year thinking – really thinking – about trauma, and the ways it might affect our bodies. The female friend I lost this year was the closest female friend I've ever had. She was a girl, and then a woman, so full of anger, jealousy and confusion due to an exceptionally difficult childhood.

Hers had been a very different childhood from mine. She came from a wealthy, large, close family, but she had lost her mother at a very young age, and the loss affected her so differently from the way my loss affected me. There was addiction – similar to what I would later experience – but there was also aggression, lying and violence; there was undeserved abuse towards those of us who showed her the very most love. The year we turned eighteen she tried to drive us both over the large concrete bridge that spanned the freezing black River Foyle because a guy she fancied had asked me if I was feeling any better. It was the first time I'd left the house since adult chickenpox had made me miss all my exams and every single party that followed. A handful of weeks later she stole another friend's phone and sent the same guy a message signed as our friend telling him that she had taken her own life because of him. The friend with the stolen phone and I had to tell him she was alive, and that none of it was even nearly true. The following year she would go on to steal my clothes and wear them in front of a guy I was seeing, noting how big they were for her. She would tie her partner up and attack him, report him to the police and try to have him deported, call his mother to say he was in prison when he wasn't, leave uni, fake her exam results and become involved with a gang of South American drug dealers. The years after this were equally as fraught and, after one final attempt to get together with my boyfriend, she dropped off the radar and I heard from her next from a convent, where she was drying out and learning to be a nun. When I broke up with my partner in Cork she rang from Spain to say she was coming to see me – she wanted to make amends. I waited and waited but she never came. Facebook showed her at party after party in South America, where she'd chosen to fly instead. When she died we were in the midst of our longest period without speaking.

I have no real knowledge of human psychology but I do know that a point comes in your life – I hope in everyone's life – when you finally accept that no one, no matter what they themselves may have suffered, should be allowed to add to *your* suffering. When she died, that friend I loved so dearly and had been hurt by so deeply, I struggled to understand how I was supposed to grieve for her. At her funeral, on Easter Sunday, buzzards and crows filled a perfect blue sky with movement. Butterflies and bees spread their promise of hope all around, and I could feel things shift inside me. Things that had been stuck for a very long time, for more than three decades; things that had less than nothing to do with that April day, and everything to do with it all in one. And so I did what I knew I needed, what I knew was the only way to get through. I went to the only thin place I had been to with her – a long, bright beach in the Gaeltacht, the Irish-speaking part of south-west Donegal.

That night, as the moon threw its light down on a sheltered, quiet harbour, inside my van, at the point where the body gives itself over into the soothing hands of sleep, I dreamed of the friend I had lost as a teenager in Ballykelly. I dreamed that gentle, kind friend I lost back then had turned into a beautiful, solitary white bird again. He was in the corner of a vast concrete warehouse, full of exceptionally violent men. He was not cowering, nor was he even in the slightest bit scared, despite the terror and the blood that was making its way onto the rough slate-grey of the dream's incarcerating walls. He was not the eighteen-year-old he had been when I last saw him. He was, instead, a little egret, serene, fearless, at one in his own white and feathered skin. I knew that he knew I was there and that we did not need to exchange any words. All the years that had passed between us since his brutal, devastating murder were not dark, then. They shone, like a celestial and brilliant light, a mirrored constellation.

The losses came in different decades from one another – they were in different lifetimes – but they wove themselves together with golden thread. Suddenly, each felt a little lighter. There was, for the very first time, a stillness inside me when I thought of them; I realised that when I closed my eyes and thought of them they were both laughing again.

It was only this summer when I began, for the first time, to talk to those closest to me about those two people I have lost. I've long struggled with honesty and intimacy in relationships of all sorts – perhaps friendship has been the hardest of all to navigate – and it felt like a laying out on the gravel of all my failings, my baggage, my loss. A way of saying: I will try to push you away. I will not tell you when I am hurt, when I need you. I am not like you; our friendship can never be easy. A way of saying: I have lost so much; only stay if you are really going to *stay*. No longer drinking has removed many of the platforms and ways to meet new friends, too, so I guess maybe I have recognised that I have to work, really work, if I want to find good people for my life.

This year I have realised that I am finding people who stay. They are coming into my path, they are seeing the sorrow, they are listening to the ache, and they are staying. They are not the kind of people that I need to try to fix. They are not people who ring me in the early hours before dawn to tell me they are going to kill themselves and then go silent for weeks afterwards. Neither are they the kind of people who criticise, ridicule, hurt, isolate, blame or abuse me. I have spent much of my life, until recently, accepting deep and disturbing abuse from the people closest to me. Recently I've been trying to unpick it, to find an order or a meaning to it all. The explanation was fairly simple, and so easy to understand. All it took was for me to admit to the certain aspects of my experience I'd been hiding from for decades. When you love people who have been through horrific times and experienced significant trauma, the balance between you can become undone. You may be made to feel – either by the person, or by your own self – that you are responsible. That you may even be to blame for their suffering. That you are not good enough. That you are not enough. That your existence is lacking in worth. These messages may be explicit – screamed at you, told to others in your life repeatedly, written in drunken emails or texts – or they may take a more covert shape, so hidden that others around you struggle to see them. You may be the only person in the whole world who your abuser treats the way they do, making it very hard to relate to others around you who do not know the other sides to them. Either way, sharing a life with people whom you love but who will not seek help for the anger that turns into abuse and is hurled at you, may leave you, first, feeling numb. Then, sooner or later, something might change inside you and you cannot and will not take it any longer. You might realise that you have changed, that you have begun to think that maybe things are not, in fact, down to you. You might see that your loved one's anger, jealousy or insecurity is not your fault. You might begin to think that maybe the treatment you have been accepting is not okay, is not right, no matter how fully you may love the person delivering it. There are many forms of abuse, and I know a handful of them. I know that if you have known abuse for a prolonged period, there may be a serious fear in you that it will never stop, and that everyone you encounter will treat you the same way: as though you have absolutely no worth. Breaking out and away is terrifying but no one – no one at all – deserves a life in which they cannot see themselves as a thing worth saving.

These days, the circle of people around me has become smaller and smaller. The friends I relied on seeing by chance, at parties, in the pub, at launches and readings – the people I only ever saw when we were all drinking and keeping our respective silences – I no longer see. I do not hear from them either. The coldness that I defined myself by for years has started, slowly but with a fierce force, to melt away, but I am only tentatively learning how to fill the gaps left over. Empty space created by the loss of many of those I once held close but I now see do not know how to step out from the cycle of abuse. Maybe someday they will, and I hope that those I am learning to live without find their own way through the pain that suffering such as ours leaves behind. For now, though, I am trying to teach myself how to trust, how to stop assuming that everyone who wants to come close will hurt me immeasurably, that they will leave me. I am trying to learn things I have never been taught. I am trying to see myself as a thing worth sticking around for.

There is laughter – there is still laughter – being sent down for me, from places I don't need to name. There is a kind of laughter, a type of joy, an enveloping from good, kind human beings – ones who accept you with all your layers of sorrow – that delivers healing.

There are things that need no language – no words – that swirl above us all, thick and black as crows, just the same on both sides of this surreal border. Like when the geese are called – up, up, and out. Then fly over, and away – back to the soil they know by heart, back to their home – and we stand, transfixed, full of something other than sorrow, other than hopelessness, other than ourselves. We stand as they fly over us, no matter where we once called home, no matter what we once knew, no matter what we have lost, on both sides of every border.

## CHAPTER SIX

### *Delicate Ghosts*

THOSE OF US WHO GROW up with a river, who spend our days – either consciously or subconsciously – mapping the course of its ethereal and surreal liquid element, lulled by its lapping, maddened by its meandering, we are shape-shifters. We are reflected and refracted. In time, as each fluid day passes, glassy and spectral, we are carried in its flow. Even those of us who have never been near to a river are affected by the water of this earth. Our insides are water and, like water, our flow is determined by things beyond our control.

Like the landscape and the seas, we too have been moulded by the past. The years have turned and battered us, held us close and then spat us out; the past has been the wildest of storms and the calmest of daybreaks all in one. We have been smoothed over like a well-worn stone. Some of us have been split; others, still, are held in the bed of the sea; some of us have beautiful holes that run right through us, a hollowed-out gap through which to see. We are the landscape, and it is us. We made our past, and it made us.

Since I returned to Derry – to the land whose suffering I still hold in a cellular, oozy place – I have found myself held by places that simply will not let me disappear under their surface. I hear the places calling to me – over and over – the pull of a moon I can never quite locate. I am often led into the sea, as if by a singing that comes from elsewhere; I swim out to meet the song, finally giving to the water all those things that were never mine to carry. In those moments of full and hauntingly cathartic surrender, when I finally lie back, sky-gaze, salt-touch, fluid-embrace, I meet myself again, as if for the first time. I own the lines and all the curves – the circle has turned, turns still, will turn always. I am in the only place I know where I am free, the place in which the silence finds the words – I am held in that delicate, beautiful and healing place, in between.

The year 2019 began with a car bomb outside the court-house. It went off just moments before a group of young local lads walked past. The only reason the bomb didn't kill or injure anyone was luck, nothing more and nothing less. I sat in a hostel in Copenhagen messaging a new English friend whose house was a stone's throw away from the bombing site. She shared how uneasy she felt talking about it all – about police escorting her into the graveyard next door and crawling like a baby on wet January ground. She thought it was 'no big deal', what she had experienced, in the light of the city's past. You who had had to live through it, she said, had been well worse off. That doesn't matter though, that doesn't take away what she and others are now being forced to go through again, two decades after the Good Friday Agreement was supposed to ensure the end of bombs, the end of people dying, the end of people losing their homes. The potential for my friend to lose her rental home, her safe haven in a city she had only just moved to, the chance that her house might be bombed – that her belongings might be burned to dust in an act of terrifying violence – is always a big deal, I think it's fair enough to say. It was only three months later that the young journalist Lyra McKee was killed during rioting in the city. Just a handful of weeks after Lyra's death, a young lad was found dead in a burnt-out car around the corner from where she was shot. Here in Derry, here in Northern Ireland, we need to trust that this is all going to stop, just as swiftly as it all started up again.

There are people living in Derry, like in many other impoverished places that have suffered vastly, who already have nothing, and who fear that the changes Brexit will bring will leave them with even less. Their lives are, and have always been, filled with plaguing, unending worry and fear, with anger and hunger, none of which they have ever been taught how to deal with.

There was *always* hunger, so much hunger. It crept up on you like a forgotten name of someone lost. The hunger was never really just about food, although the city has had a shortage of that for many centuries. We simply never had enough – enough of *anything* – to feel like we were *real*. I hated it. I hated that sense of longing – that craving – that feeling of losing, being repeated over and over and over. I watched as funding was cut for almost every good thing that came to the city, as people talked about unemployment and poverty – about how we all left once we'd got our education, how everyone always left. Mental health funding, hostels for alcohol and drug addicts, suicide prevention groups: cuts to services this city really – desperately – needs. Loss is not an easy thing to live alongside. The way the city of Derry has continually seemed set on breaking itself up even further made me angry for decades. My city seemed to be in permanent self-destruct mode. It felt to me, even as a teenager, that we must somehow have deserved the nothingness that we had been given. That somewhere, far back, we must have done something so awful that our city was being punished: an ancient archaic penance. TV, films, the radio, they were all full of places where life seemed to be following a different – easier – path. A path where good things could and did happen. Where you could choose to stay in your hometown, free from fear, free from hunger for something more – something easier, something safe. Other places seemed like places where people weren't always being forced to leave, where people could choose to stay.

At what point does a thing cease to be whole? How much breakdown does it take to bring you to breaking point, to broken point? When does a city become merely a severed ghost of itself?

When Mum moved away to Edinburgh, my brother and I moved back to Derry to live with our granny and granda until we finished our exams. It was a temporary fix – when my A-Levels were done I was heading off to university, and that would really and truly be the end of that period of my life, those early years moving from place to place, and never really sure how to get through. I hadn't even seen the house my mum and her then husband were moving into, and I knew that I would never live there anyway as I was setting off into solo, adult life that year. I was very close to my grandparents but the house they were living in at that time wasn't the one they had lived in for most of my life, so it felt a wee bit unknown too, like I was really only passing through. So, at just-turned-seventeen, I tried to accept that the desire for a 'home' – somewhere I felt safe, at ease, like I belonged – was something I needed to let go of.

I remember so clearly the afternoon at school when I realised that if I stood any chance at making a secure life for myself, it was going to mean really working – working as hard as I could possibly manage. And so I started. I studied every single day, for as long as I could, and as hard as I could. I was in an exceptionally competitive grammar school, and I joined the Oxbridge group, all of us battling it out to get the best grades, to have the most interesting personal letter for our applications; even then I felt like an outsider constantly. I had never had, and never would have, the same background as the others. Silence became my way out. I didn't feel anchored, even when I was with really kind people; I felt, always, too much on the periphery to really step inside – to really get close and make proper, lasting friendships. It became the resounding theme of my relationships – all of them. At work, with partners and friends, when you know you are keeping back so very much about your background and experiences, hiding away who you are, it is hard to see how any real intimacy could be created.

I worked as hard as I could to get the grades I needed to get into Trinity College Dublin, where I studied English Literature and Classical Civilisation. I hadn't realised it at the time but this move across the border was possibly the most meaning-laden event of my life. The decision – almost a non-decision in how casually I made it – reflected the need in me, the want. A want for things to be different, just. For the past to loose its bleeding and bloodied grip. For the marks left imprinted on me to fade, even just a little bit – enough to make me feel human.

As seems to so often be the way with me, the move came wrapped up tightly in difficulties and weirdness. A week before my exams began – a few months after my brother and I had moved into my granny and granda's house – I contracted adult chickenpox. I woke up one night to a blinding headache and the oddest type of queasiness. The next morning I was covered in chickenpox for the second time in my life, something I was fairly sure just didn't happen. My skin was like a foreign land. Trying to study in that level of pain was hard going, to say the least. My memories of those last months at school – *not* at school, rather – are of my granda coaxing me from sleep to learn sections of Virgil's *Aeneid* off by heart. Of him sitting up with me into the wee small hours learning about the history of nationalism and unionism on our island, the Romantic poets and women in the Greek world. I sat all my exams in my grandparents' kitchen – my sick breaks in the bathroom being timed, the lovely study warden taking the boxes of tablets in my granny's cupboard apart, searching for cheat notes that weren't there. I managed, somehow, to get the grades and I was well enough – only just – to start my degree when I was due to, that October.

I had planned to move in with my friend from school, whose dad had bought her a flat in Dublin, and to whom I had already paid the deposit. But she had already started to suffer at the hands of mental illness. I hadn't seen her for most of the summer, and when I did see her, just a month before we were due to embark on our university life together, she was more unrecognisable than I'd been that summer. Anorexia and bulimia, combined with a harsh daily exercise regime, had left her a frail shell of herself. The hardest part to process though was the change in her personality. The person I knew and loved, I hoped, was still there – underneath a confused knot of self-hatred. I only fully understood when she died, this spring, that she'd spent half of her life battling with her own self, with parts of herself that scared her. I am still trying to find ways to honour the girl I knew and loved before that summer we turned eighteen. She started, that summer, to take the actions and words of those *she* knew and loved, and twist them in on themselves – like an eel hauled from the belly of the sea, out of place and lost in translation. She went from begging me to live with her – she would die if I didn't – to wanting to leave her options open – she might want to leave the room empty for all the new friends she would meet on her course. My stomach flipped and rocked, fearful and stuck at the in-between parts of her storm. Next her dad wanted her to live alone so he could visit to check up on her – I had no idea what each new day would bring as I packed my books into boxes, leaving the address section for delivery unwritten. Finally, the week of moving came. My friend's dad rang me on my granny's landline and told me under no circumstances was I to move in with his sick daughter. I had to listen, of course. I had to abandon a friend I loved dearly, for her own – and my own – good. I see now that this, the starting of my adult life, came wrapped in as much confusion, fear and worry about the idea of 'home' as any time before it. Moving out on my own had always felt, when I'd imagined it, to be the answer: the point when it would all ease and I would find safe harbour, feel rooted. The line I was walking was the same line I'd always walked, except this time I was utterly alone.

My student loan didn't come through in time and I now had nowhere organised to live. All of the signs seemed pointed towards the idea that Dublin wasn't meant to be, but I buried my head deep and carried on. My dad, who I had not seen properly for years by then, decided all out of nowhere that he wanted to drive me and my stuff to Dublin. I'm still not really sure where that came from, why he wanted to do it, but in letting him, I was learning to be softer; I was making room inside. Our family unit had broken so devastatingly I think we all still bear the scars decades later. Perhaps my turning eighteen – twice the age I was when he left us – triggered something in him, created a gap that he felt he might be able to dip through, to take the first steps towards getting to know his first-born child again.

I didn't hear from Dad again for most of my four years at university, though, and for many years afterwards. We only really found a way to communicate as the strangers we had become when I was in my late twenties, living in Edinburgh. The path we learned to walk towards a shared future was not an easy one, and we still have much work to do, but I am willing to trust – and trust is such a gift.

It seemed a fruitless search, half of my life ago, trying to find somewhere affordable to live in Dublin, and I only had the limited funds I'd managed to save and some that I'd borrowed from my grandparents until my loan finally came through weeks later. My boss at my part-time job knew a woman who was renting out rooms, miles out of Dublin city centre, and I jumped at that straight away. And so, one early October Sunday, my father collected me and my boxes and drove us across the border – crossing lines both invisible and contemptuous, surreal and unbelievable – into my adult life in Dublin.

Dublin was both all I had imagined it would be and, at the same time, constantly shifting, its anonymous otherness seemed born afresh each day. I loved my course but something about the whole beautifully ancient city just didn't quite fit; I didn't fit. I wandered around, wraith-like, trying to make my soles slot neatly into the ghost footprints left by those before me – traces of lost souls – dragging themselves over cobblestones, through infamous landmarks and along the Liffey. But I could never drop the feeling of deep sadness I felt. I watched as friends went 'home' for weekends and study leave, and I was able to go to my grandparents, of course, but it just never felt like anywhere was really *my* place; nowhere felt like home. I always thought that it was jealousy that I felt towards my classmates, that stinging sense of them having something that kept them in place in the world, allowing their sense of self to take root. But now I don't think it was jealousy; the way I felt wasn't just about me or what I felt I didn't have. The world just didn't seem fair, and I didn't know how to make it all change. In my family we walked on eggshells around each other. There was so much pain, and none of us had been shown how to talk about it. Silence took over, which – although better than shouting, threats and broken bonds – is utterly detrimental, and exceptionally hard to untangle yourself from. Not being allowed to voice your pain, being told you are misremembering or are wrong, being made to feel like you have no right to move on, that your suffering is less valid – your hurt of less worth – leaves you in a place it feels near impossible to crawl back from.

I moved every few months as the rent in Dublin went up – I lived there at the height of the 'Celtic Tiger', making the city even more difficult to manage – and worked long hours alongside studying, jostling to keep up with classmates who could afford to keep renting their flats over the summer, go away at weekends exploring, go on holidays together to Italian villas during the Easter break. It began to grind me down – every single bit of it – leaving dusty trails of resentment at my tired feet. I hated myself for feeling that way. Those first few years I was in Dublin the whole new world of social media had sprung up in full force. I didn't have a laptop, so it all felt a little odd to me; I stayed on the outside of its alien perimeters and watched as my classmates grew closer, this time from different rooms, buildings, countries. I could never afford somewhere to live in a good, safe area, so I ended up living in ten different flats – each more or less as bad as the other – during the four years I was at university. They were often spaces where I didn't even really want to sleep, let alone spend any waking hours. Lots of my time was spent in Trinity – at lectures and in the library – and the bulk of the rest of it was spent working in the jobs I needed in order to scrape by. Most people I knew who worked did one or two shifts so they could go to gigs, for dinner or to save for travelling in the long summers off. The differences between my lived experience and that of my classmates seemed to widen and widen as time went by. One of the girls in my circle of friends struggled so much to believe that I really was supporting myself through uni (aside from my student loan – which wouldn't have even paid my rent) that she genuinely thought I just didn't want to be her friend when I refused to go out salsa dancing for the third Friday in a row. Eventually she grasped the fact that I worked every single weekend night throughout university, apart from the one she talked me into taking off to celebrate her twenty-first.

Now I see how much easier it would have been if I'd felt comfortable sharing my background a bit more honestly, if I had just stopped trying to pretend I was a different person from the one I was. The more I noticed how my classmates' lives compared to mine, the more I retreated into my own shell. For quite some time I had tried to carefully mould myself and my past into the outlines they all shared; no matter where they came from there seemed to be a bright, common thread that ran through their pasts like a beacon. I could see it – that thing that they had all shared together but I couldn't decipher the language it spoke. I tried to shape the words, words that would explain why I might seem a little different from them all, but they caught on the insides of my gums; the truths I was scared to share hid in the enamel of my teeth. I searched for ways to try to explain the kind of life I had lived – growing up always ready to leave, on alert, scared all the time and never really sure what the things I was feeling were called, or how to make them stop. I was a grown adult but I spent every day in Dublin feeling like a lost, scared child. It had all come too quickly and with no real help, proper planning or support. Suddenly I was in the second stage of my life, with no idea how to make it all work, how to make the sorrow ease.

I didn't realise it back then, like lots of things we often are blind to at the time, but even from those very early days of being properly on my own in the world, I sought solace in whichever safe spaces I could find outside. I wasn't that wee girl with her microscope and her worrying silence in that concrete Derry back garden any longer, but I was still just as scared. I was still as lost. If anything, in fact, things had got worse – the fear had magnified, and my silence, born decades earlier, and nurtured ever since, like a promise made, was still thick as ice, and even more unbreakable.

I gave up trying to fit in. I gave in to the blurred beat of the past, its echoes reaching the surface, still, no matter how much I tried to muffle them.

I studied hard, and worked harder again, in jobs I hated and that left me bone-tired and only just managing to pay my bills. I worked various daytime jobs – delivering flyers for nightclubs, raising money on the street for children with a condition that made their skin as fragile as a butterfly's, selling at markets, and other things I know I must have done but have lost from my memory. I worked nights in a hotel a short walk from the canal for most of my time at university, finishing my shifts anywhere between three and six in the morning on Thursday, Friday and Saturday nights.

Looking back, I see how important that canal was for me during those frightening, confusing times. I walked alongside it – close enough to imagine I could hear the stories it had been told over centuries: tales, like mine, of loss and shame, of weeping and of helplessness. The swans filled my dreams, the dreams that came in those funny hours between hazy dawn and the point when the light drips fully back into the world. The dream swans were often exactly like their real selves when I walked along beside them: necks entwined, heads covering dirtied white bodies on a messy nest, in the shade of tall rushes, silent and at peace. Sometimes, though, they were vicious – much wilder than any city swan I have ever known: ice-plumed and violent, talking and singing, turning the canal world into one of myth and gothic layering for fleeting, sleeping moments. I began to find myself at the canal at moments other than those when I carried my tired body back from sweaty, dirty nightclubs. I took myself to those swans in the dimpled, dappled mornings when I felt at a loss for how to bring myself to the library, to the lectures, to the coffee breaks with the others that I couldn't afford. I watched them at different times of day, in all of the seasons; I watched them as the years of my early adulthood spun by. I saw that the canal was home to other creatures, too, many that I had never known existed in the same world as I did. It was mostly the birds that drew me close – the coots and the ducks, the thin-necked black cormorants, the geese that came and left in the sky above. But there were other things, too – rats and a single shy otter, two types of dragonfly and mayflies – so many mayflies. Butterflies and moths, too. The canal held me tightly, kept me as safe as it kept all of its other creatures in turn. It didn't take long until I started to imagine the other places in this new, unknown city that might be able to make me feel the same way – safe for a handful of hours, my mind temporarily quietened, my body at unfamiliar ease. I went where I could just about afford on public transport, or places I could walk to. I ignored the signs that spoke of pollution on the littered strand at Sandymount, directly across from tall towers spewing out smoke, only slightly greyer than the sky it was being exhaled into. The bees that hummed through the grasses and flowers at the verges, the high-up Vs of migrating geese, the oystercatchers and turnstones – redshank and dunlin – I knew *these* things were keeping me away from a risk of a much more dangerous kind than any toxins that the sand held in its shards.

I spent lots of time by the sea but never in it during my

time in Dublin – countless walks along strands during sun and rain, hikes up Killiney Hill, and others I knew no name for in sleet and snow, as tears of struggle and exhaustion stung my cheeks. I remember lots of afternoons in Howth and Dun Laoghaire. I remember lighthouses and Martello towers, boats and ships, graveyards full of ivy and beautiful names kept in stone; I remember the sense that I was learning how to keep myself as visible as these things – the sense that I was filling my days as a means of making sure I stuck around.

I left Dublin as soon as I could – just like I left Derry and just like I would leave countless places in my future. In the summer before my final year at uni, I met a man who wanted to look after me. It all happened very quickly – he had an intoxicating singsong Cork accent, he didn't flinch when I talked of my past, and he asked no questions. We had been together – long-distance – for only a handful of months when I realised that something was wrong – very wrong – inside my body. The pain I'd been ignoring for months had finally become unbearable, and by the time I went to see a doctor I could barely walk and was bleeding my insides out at a rapid speed. I didn't know it back then, but I would go on to have so much of those insides cut out that it would change the path of my life irrevocably. I would lose so much blood and lining. Each time cells were cut out that shouldn't have been there it felt a little less real than the last. I felt a little less real, in turn.

I spent lots of my final year at uni *not* at uni, mirroring my final year at school. I moved into the flat my partner lived in in Cork after I had my first round of surgery in Derry, travelling up and down to Dublin when I could. I managed, somehow, to graduate with the grade I'd been hoping for. By that point, I was unrecognisable to my own self, just as I had been after the chickenpox, except this time the changes to my form were on the inside as well as the outside.

Just before my first operation, I was cleaning the kitchen of my flat by the canal. A sound made its way up off the floor of the utility room, along the kitchen and into ears that well remembered having heard such a call before. A wild river rat had made its way into the house, this time not cradled in my brother's little boy's hands, but of its own accord. My mind meandered back that grey afternoon, standing in a cold kitchen in the middle of Dublin city centre, to another kitchen in another city across the Irish border. We spent a while locked in each other's presence, a spell of our own doing. It was so calm, the rat – not seeming out of place at all – rather as if we both had slipped between worlds, at ease in our individual places. At ease, even for a brief moment, in our own creaturely forms, too – no matter what anyone else may have thought of our bodies; our blood pumping beneath our skins; inside our in-between and fractured landscapes. Home, the idea of it, the thought of ever feeling safe, lost all of its weighty, scary sense in that moment. That rat, and that odd, calm moment, was a gift: a way of entering into another place, somewhere where I felt like I belonged.

## CHAPTER SEVEN

### *Frozen Bones*

EVERY SINGLE TIME I CONJURE Cork up in my mind, every single time I remember that city in the other corner of this island from Derry, I hear the humbling, beautiful echoing of bells.

I had moved to Cork as I was in too much pain from surgery to stay alone in Dublin, and things were not secure or solid enough for me to move in with my mum and brothers in the council house they had just moved into. They had all just left Wales, where they had been living to accommodate mum's new husband – the leaving of whom they were all trying to deal with now that they were back in Derry. If I'm honest, I remember thinking that the further south I went the easier my past experiences in the north might be to swallow. As if they might find it easier to make themselves hidden in my guts. My partner was a man who I see now made me feel as bad about myself as *I* made me feel about myself, and that was really saying something. It seems such a devastating, unfair reality that often those of us who have suffered abuse of one or other form meet abuse again and again, in different forms throughout our lives. I imagined a pattern made by invisible birds that flew above my head, signalling in ways I could not help.

Cork was an edge-land place for me. I was at an in-between stage – not quite finished university, not quite in the real world, not quite healed. I wandered the outskirts of its beating heart – alone and hopeless – scared of the emptiness I couldn't quite drown.

My partner was the coldest person I had ever met. He never hurt me as such, there was just no warmth, no real understanding. It was like sharing a close life with a complete stranger. It felt safe, that ice that kept us held together in the same flat, but was too thick to let us really get to know one another. I had grown colder, too. I knew I wanted nothing more than someone, somewhere, something – anything – to make me feel that I was going to be okay, but I had no clue how to make that happen. We worked long hours, apart, he and I. He spent lots of time with his family – one that wanted nothing to do with someone from a broken family like mine – and I grew more at ease with the dark feelings that, at the beginning, had shocked me to my core. I started to wake up, not just once or twice a month like before, but every single day, with suicidal thoughts.

At first I was angry with myself for even daring to feel that way. The woman who had brought me into the world had spent years telling me that I would never really know what true suffering meant. Telling me that, due to the vast sacrifices she had made to keep me safe – leaving her family and the place she called home – I had escaped the suffering that she herself alone had experienced, that which she deemed real and true suffering. I had not lost my family, she told me over and over. I had not been left alone in this world; I had got lucky. From the year I turned sixteen, my mother spent much of the time she chose to be in my life telling me that the pain I had suffered was not real, was not valid. On any of the few occasions I had tried to speak with her about how I felt, of the darkness I could never shake off, she voiced her own story – one that left no room for mine to exist on the same page.

And so I believed those things: that what had happened had in some way been my fault. I learned to hate myself more and more, in a variety of intricate ways. And why wouldn't I? Look at what I'd grown up through, bits of death embedded in my skin, violence creeping up from shrouded places, no sense of normality anywhere, really, nowhere at all. I knew I couldn't undo it – any of it – I couldn't swap its darkness for light, make it into a thing much less heavy than it was. And so what was the point? What was the point in anything, at all? Things had become increasingly difficult since they'd moved back to Derry for my mum and my wee brothers. She had gone through her second divorce, and this time was no easier than the first. I had no money, no support, just worry and the fear that nothing was ever, ever going to change. I could count on a fifth of a hand the times I'd heard from my father since I'd left Derry. My partner was becoming increasingly distant. *What was the point of it all?*

Breaking the silence about darkness – like thinking about

it – is a very hard thing indeed. There is a weight around your neck that is much more than just yours to bear. That weight seems, at times, so feathery as to be wholly insubstantial. So light and full of nothing that you would feel ashamed to even whisper of it to another; much heavier is the weight carried by so many others. We seem set, here, as in many places, on disallowing ourselves to own our own suffering. Shame keeps us silent. I had grown up in a family and a city that had watched suffering ripple through their lines like an unstoppable wave; almost every single person I knew had suffered more than me. I knew that my ache, my darkness, the black crow inside my guts, paled into insignificance against that which everyone else seemed to be forced to carry. My trauma wasn't hard enough earned to even try to voice it. 'You think *you've* had it hard; how do you think *I* feel?' And so you let the silence deepen, you watch it grow and ricochet across the surface of the land and sea. You bury the crow inside you deeper, deeper still, so deep that even *you* can pretend he isn't there.

In Cork it was even more effortless to remain anonymous, oddly, despite it being a much smaller city, and the people more tightly knit. The folk were held closely together by family and history, like an old Aran cardigan. I have never experienced families and groups of friends closer to each other than in Cork. No one I lived or worked with seemed to mind whether I wanted to get to know them or not, and I didn't have enough confidence to ask to spend time with the people I met. I found it so hard to integrate at all because of anxiety, and I became more used to being on my own.

My sorrow had begun, by then, to spread itself out underneath my skin like a dark blanket – unbearably heavy. I felt the weight of sadness under, rather than on, my chest. Loneliness and the sharp edges of loss were trying to get out from in beside my ribs. I was in my mid twenties by that stage, and had experienced repeated invasive surgery, each time feeling myself become more and more removed from my own body. I could never afford to take time off work, which in itself meant that I worked through physical pain, and wasn't really close enough to anyone to talk about it. Colleagues would joke about needing a translator to understand me – my Derry accent was broad, concrete – and they struggled to read between its singsong cadences. I had found myself so far from the border but still the sorrow of the North dragged behind me like an echo.

It seems now like such a fitting analogy; I couldn't speak in any way that made people understand what was happening, how sad and lonely I was feeling. I buried words like bog-oak beneath frozen, unstable ground.

Cork is a city that has witnessed her own fair share of violence; the red of her Rebel County flag is a hard-earned one. Nonetheless, that far south in the island, the North still feels like a foreign land to many people. In Cork I found brand new ways to forget, to conceal, to disappear. I realised only recently that after leaving Derry, all the places I ran to had one thing in common: I could get to water within a handful of moments. Cork's source was the River Lee. The city was actually founded on the flat, swampy islands on the Lee, remembered in its name *Corcaigh Mhór Mumhain* – 'The Great Marsh of Munster'. The core branch of the river rises in Gougane Barra, a wee secluded valley nestled in the Shehy Mountains where streams and rivulets flow down the steep sides of a glacial canyon, filling a lake. The Lee is associated with St Finbarr, who is said to have closely followed the river from its source to the city where he laid the foundations of his monastery. Like Cork's saint, I too spent much of my time there mapping the flow of the River Lee – lulled from howling over into sleep by its ancient lapping too many times to recall. It felt so different from the River Foyle: softer, younger, less defined by unstoppable and ferocious hunger.

Peering back on this period, it is a muted, foggy scene I find, as if everything back there is coated in grey dust that won't quite shift. I have deep, almost cinematic memories of stone – grey and sacred, scattered long back but still suffused with the very same meaning that they always have held, in circles and covering holes – markers and reminders in the green, humming land. I spent lots of time on the edges of the county – Sheep's Head Peninsula, Crow Head on the Beara Peninsula, Dingle, Kinsale, Schull – I had so much time to wander, and I went as far as I possibly could, across the county border into Kerry, too. North, west, east and south of County Cork – climbing heights in snowfall that I could never have imagined I would manage, and even now I wonder if the photographs taken at the top of mountains are real. I wonder if there is any of the girl in those snowy, blurry photographs still there inside me, and if she would recognise me in herself if we could ever stand there at the top side by side, as individual white flakes came to rest upon our faces.

For many years I carried gorse from the Caha Mountains and heather from the sea cliffs at Crow Head – each gathered on days when I felt sure I was at the end of my own line, thoughts of suicide never too far from my days. The gorse and the heather both faded over the seasons that they bore witness to inside the pocket of my old green work jacket. Each became a dried-out reminder of that achingly beautiful, haunting land-scape, of that part of my life I was convinced I wouldn't make it through. I lost them on the move back to Derry years later, along with a handful of other things that never showed up on the other side: a blue woollen blanket from a charity shop on the Isle of Mull, a tall earthenware mug with the word 'North' inscribed at the bottom, bought at a car boot sale in Edinburgh one Sunday morning, and a mobile of paper whooper swans I'd had in every rented room I'd ever occupied since that one in Cork city. When those things never turned up, the first thing that came to mind was a wet, windy visit to Allihies, to see the white rock that the Children of Lir are said to be buried beneath. On that day, the hurt I was wakening to every single day – the self-hatred and the thought that I would be better off just lying down and not getting back up – felt like it had reached the lowest point possible. My grief, like Lir's children, was buried beneath a single white rock and I didn't know where, if anywhere, I was supposed to turn.

I carried on, trying to pretend that everything was okay while that other part of me, the angry, scared, worried part, got worse and worse. I found myself weeping all the time, and I had no idea why and even less idea how to make it stop. I was prescribed antidepressants which I took. They made me sick, and the sense of not quite being in my own body strengthened, grew limbs. I was looking down on my own body from above. I was looking down. I was looking down, and then one day I was ready to swallow, to run, to jump in. In Cork I tried to take my own life four times. After the last of these attempts, I knew I had to leave. I left my partner, and Cork, a week later, and never went back.

Being honest about depression – about suicidal thoughts, about wanting to let that weight take you down so far that you don't ever resurface – is absolutely terrifying. Many of us remain silent – unsure how to even begin to bring the words to the surface. Sometimes, a moment comes when you are forced out of silence – when the gag you have tied around yourself is cut. I had finally got to a stage where I understood that the past was not only drastically affecting my present but that it held the power to put an end to my future. I no longer wanted to be in this world, one that I loved so dearly but that I just didn't feel I could take any more from. I had taken enough. Everything, every single part of being alive, had carried such sorrow and pain, and growing older wasn't easing it, not even a tiny bit. I may have moved away from my childhood, and from the Troubles of my home but I certainly hadn't left any of it behind. I was more than sad now; rather, I was less than sad: I had reached a point where I had swiftly started to stop feeling anything. I had become numb, and now I realise that this was the most unsafe place of all the places I had ever been.

The darker the thoughts got, the more convinced I was that I needed to go further away from Ireland, further away from the past. Running was the only choice I ever really felt I had. It was the only thing I knew, the only course of action I had ever been shown. I left Cork on the day I decided that I would go. My graduation was due to take place that week but I did not even have the money for the bus to Dublin, let alone to rent a gown. I stayed at my mum's and worked myself to the bone for a handful of months until I had saved enough money to make a move away from my island. I'd always been drawn to the Scottish landscape – so much like home but with what I saw as more opportunity and space to heal and to grow.

I moved to Edinburgh, made friends who knew very little of the Troubles of my homeland, found a job that took up every bit of my time and all of my energy. I dragged my coal-black crow of sorrow around like a body in a sack. Now that I was no longer on the island that had broken me, I felt as if I had been offered a rebirth, of a form – a chance to make myself into a thing as light as a candle, as a feather. We are so good at telling ourselves stories that have no feet on solid land. In Scotland, as in Ireland, I sought out wild, ancient and healing places, places that felt full of the promise of new growth. I started swimming outdoors again, as regularly as I had in childhood. I swam in many bodies of water, found stones that made my hands vibrate on touch, zigzagged my way up hills and down mountains, journeyed from island to island, trying desperately to fill my lungs with the fullness of being alive.

In the daytime, in normal everyday life, during the distracting grind of working Monday to Friday to pay for my Steiner teacher training degree at the weekends, all was fine. I felt like I'd found a safe future for myself through teaching – secure and of my own making. All would be okay now, I promised myself. Then night would come and the veil would slip away. No matter how busy I was, no matter what my life entailed, no matter how much better things looked, finally, on the outside, my inside was still a tangled, knotted mess. I still hated myself.

All I wanted was to take the way I was feeling and whittle it, to shape it into a thing that I could live alongside and grow to accept, somehow. I would go on visits to Ireland – each of my parents had by then settled within walking distance of where we'd been petrol-bombed. My dad's second marriage had ended too. Things that have been broken and have never been allowed to properly heal, never been put back together properly are riddled with invisible but devastating faultlines. My family has not been a unit for decades. Suffering and sorrow, when not worked through, lead to anger, resentment and aggression. Or to coldness, lack of contact and burying your head in the ground. It is hard – so hard – to try to imagine a way that any of those things could ever be avoided, given what so many of us in the North had to live through.

Then, in the year I turned twenty-eight, I began to really and properly break down. It happened slowly at first, then became more and more rapid, without me being able to even attempt to stop it. I would go to work, come home, and straight away close my bedroom curtains and try to pretend the world wasn't still happening out there. If I stopped going out, seeing people, going places, then time would freeze, and I would have no more worries about my unstable, scary future. If I could just try to stop the present moment, then the past didn't really exist any more, either; it would become a place that I had never known. I started drinking that year. I see it now, when I have the grace of hindsight, as the ultimate form of giving up: giving up respect for myself, giving up any sense of belief that things might get better, giving up hope. My late twenties went by in the blink of an eye. When my thirties arrived, I realised I didn't know how to put the pieces of myself back together. There were holes and gaps, like the barren interior of Donegal. Cracks ran the whole way through the map of my insides.

# PART TWO

*Feather and Stone*

## CHAPTER EIGHT

## *Found Things*

HOW FAR BACK, ALONG THE line that is not straight, the line that is not marked, the line that is invisible to our eyes, must we travel, to find the source? Where does the past cease?

Where does it stop?

And when?

*Where do you end?*

*Where do I begin?*

*Where do you end, and I begin?*

Where does the cycle start? Where does the moon take her first white and whispered breaths? When does the sea move away from the land?

Where does the story step off the page, hope-bright, feather-white, beneath a blackened, moth-light sky?

Silence, like the moon, is a white circle moving through the seasons, shape-shifting its way across the phases of its own darkness.

There are places that speak of that unwritten language of

letting go, of giving in, of being held like a hand in silent, universal prayer.

•

When I left Ireland I vowed never to live on her shores again. I said that I would absolutely never live in Derry again, least of all on the side of the river on which I experienced the deepest trauma. I spent fifteen years living away from Derry, running from place to place, dragging the things I'd seen around with me, like a shadow too bulky for its mirrored form. Today, I live within walking distance of the places I ran away from. Less than a minute's walk from my current house, just around the corner, a British soldier was shot dead six feet in front of me. His face entered my dreams – year after year after year, even though I'm fairly certain I would not have seen it with my own eyes. I was six years old. I was coming home from school with my mum, baby brother five days shy of turning four, and the wee boy who lived across the street from us on our housing estate. The whole thing happened quicker than the blink of an eye. We were back home in our own kitchen drinking strong, sugary tea before I could even try to find the source of all the noise. I dreamed of him for decades, that lost soldier. I saw his face in the most troubled of nights. Who would have thought the murder of an armed stranger could wound as deeply as that of a friend? I haven't seen the soldier's face even once this year. I carried the memory of him as I swam the length of the cove at Inch Island a wee while back, and as I pushed against the waves I knew that I was letting go – of his face, and of so much else that came before him, and after – and I wondered what had got me to this point. I hope that others who have known such loss have got there too, to a still, gentle point, and that they feel hope again, that they look to the sky and see a way through.

Leaving Ireland is a story that was written for us many moons back, long before we were born. This story of feeling displaced, disjointed – lost – is the story so many other people from my home share. We are a people who mostly live in lands not our own, caught in the in-between places, never quite fully landed on any shore. I played my part in this shared story from a very young age. I am still playing my part, three years after I returned to Irish shores. We have never been able to stay. We have been forced away, by poverty and violence, by loss and by lack. Ireland has been sending her people elsewhere for centuries. Canada, America, Australia, the UK, Europe and almost every spot on this earth have taken these people in, have held them close, have tried to keep them safe, have tried to stop their emigrant tears from flooding back to the body of water they know the best.

Most of my limited free time in Scotland was spent exploring the islands of the west of my adopted homeland. I returned again and again to the Isle of Mull, gravitating to the north-west of that wild island. I stayed at Treshnish, just around the bay from Calgary in a safe yet dramatic nook of wilderness. The view, on a day free of the hauntingly beautiful haar – a sea fog that creeps in from the furthermost reaches of the

Atlantic – takes in the eerily remarkable Treshnish Isles. When night falls in that place, the world around you is so black and still that it is as if the world is holding her breath, waiting for the silence to seep right into your very bones, waiting for tranquillity. I swam in all of the icy-cold bodies of water around me and gathered ancient stones from the inner belly of a waterfall I have only ever found once, unable to find my way back to its clear waters no matter how hard I try. On the third time I visited Treshnish, I realised that when I arrived at the bottom field of the farm, when I saw the Treshnish Isles peek through the thick grey mist, when I heard the sea against the sand at Calgary Bay, I was experiencing the deepest sense of calm and ease I maybe ever had before. That feeling, the one that drew me back to the Isle of Mull again and again, that lingered even days after returning to Edinburgh, was about something deep-rooted, something that was happening underneath my skin. No matter where I went on the Isle of Mull, no matter who came with me – more especially when I was completely on my own – I was being held in place by something I could never quite put my finger on; I was being soothed and nourished by an unnameable thing.

The thing that was drawing me back, pulling me in close, giving me a sense of hope for the first time in years, was the *place*. Something happened to me every single time I returned to the farm where I stayed in Treshnish. When I went to bed at night, unlike the sleeplessness and anxiety that met me in other places, I slept the whole night long, like a baby. I slept and I dreamed beautiful, nourishing dreams. In one dream that stays in my memory, I was standing in a wee clearing, not unlike a copse I had found in another part of the island, close to the ferry port. I thought I was completely on my own but I suddenly realised I was being watched, and that the watcher did not have a human form. I was sharing the place, sharing the dream, with an exquisite hummingbird. As it darted about, weaving in and out of view, I became aware of yet another presence in the dream – an old man I had never seen in real life. He told me that the choice was mine. If I left the bird, I could be the one to claim the discovery of it (it was a bird that had not been seen by human eyes before) but then I would not get to really *see* the bird, and I might never again. I have never experienced that dream again but the vision comes back to me, over and over in this waking world, a kaleidoscopic echo.

There are places on the Isle of Mull and in other parts of the Celtic world that we still have no means to comprehend; traces of meaning have been left but not in any language we are still rooted enough to decipher. Memorials – made by humans – have been marking thin places on this earth for thousands of years. Ancient people, especially in Ireland and Britain, were forever marking spaces as sacred and worth remembering, as if to say, to whoever might be listening, whenever they might come along: *this place is a place to hold close, a place that will hold you close, if you let it*.

I spent most of my free time in Scotland outside and completely alone just like I had in every other place I had settled before. Sometimes a friend and their partner, their children maybe, might walk with me here and there but I mostly spent my days in the wild, howling landscape of Scotland by myself. It is only really this year that I see how much of an accidental gift that ended up being.

The flat I shared was on the Meadows – a green part of the city in the middle of a handful of affluent areas and student streets. Lots of local residents nurtured gardens in ways that encouraged insects and birds, foxes and other creatures, and so even if I could only manage a walk across the Meadows, on days when my body was weary with the sadness I couldn't throw off, it was enough to bring a wee glimmer of something light into a day otherwise full of something dark. I walked alone through ancient woodlands – across the Hermitage of Braid, up Blackford Hill and down again, around the pictur-esque old city, and then up to the very height of an extinct volcano. A volcano visible from my bedroom window which I watched turn every colour under the sun during various moments of alcohol-bathed, suicidal thoughts. A volcano I slipped from during thick January snowfall, after seeing a peregrine falcon for the first time.

I walked the Pentland Hills, listening out for bells, long hidden in the belly of a loch. I made my way across bodies of water to every island I could manage. On the Isle of Bute I watched a crow gather sticks to build its nest for so long that I missed my ferry back. I remember caring so little about this inability to return to my everyday life. At Rosslyn Chapel I lay beneath an oak and cried salty, unbecoming tears – thinking of all the sorrows from another place, with other oaks, as a nuthatch kept my weepy company for long enough that my face grew dry.

I began to gather more things from the places I sought refuge in, and to bring them into my rented home. My two large windowsills, looking out across the Meadows on the right-hand side and Arthur's Seat on the left, filled up with all manner of objects varying in size and texture, depending on where I had found them. I mostly found those things on stretches of sand alongside the sea: shards and fragments, smithereens and bits and bobs, parts and portions of the coastline that was keeping me safe back then. Stones and pebbles, feathers and sea-glass, bones and sticks brought back with me, from one place, to lie in another: why? Were they bringers of comfort and constancy, these hallowed, found things? Even after being spat out – dislodged from wherever they had once been, left to lie in the dark and cold – even after weathering storm after storm, there was still a place for them. There was a place for them in my home, in my life and in my day, and even back then I knew that meant something, even if I didn't know what. Did they make me feel a wee bit more embedded – in place, in a life I was struggling with every day, in my own body, that vessel that was somehow still dragging me through? Like those pieces, those measures of time and place – of memory – I was still there, too. I was still visible. I was still holding on.

I was hearing the call of the sea more forcefully than ever before, and I obeyed its pleas to draw close. All along the coastline of Scotland, right down to the border it shares with England – and across it, I threw my thin, tired body into the waves. I swam beneath cliffs of the sea and birds of the same. I swam in grey, churning waves, and in water so calm it lay on the surface as if it were a limestone lough. I swam in the sea that bordered islands, the sea that lay far from any dwelling, the sea where there were so many other people around that I blended into the background like a grain of sand. I travelled over it in boats and ferries, too, and watched creatures of the sky I had only before seen in books. I camped on dunes, and in trees and in places that haunted my sleep. The Farne Islands, Hadrian's Wall, the Hebrides, Dorset, Kent, the west coast of Scotland, and more and more and more. I ran and ran and ran; I ran to places that would hold me, like a thing worth being held.

I started to feel a little better, finally. I felt that if I managed to keep going as I was, I would – I could – make it through. Maybe it was the sheer fact of growing older, of realising that you simply cannot move against the river, no matter how much you would like to alter its flow. Perhaps it was the fact that I was learning acceptance – not of my own self, yet, that would take many more years – rather, of the fact that sometimes things just are unfair. Sometimes life is hard for some people, most, if not all of the time. Maybe it had a bit to do with the weather in Scotland. The longer I stayed there, the more I realised that there simply was no point in making solid plans. Trips to islands could be cancelled by spring snowfall, camping plans scuppered by heavy downpour in the height of summer; entire festivals – months in the planning – could be called off because the weather was not on your side. Maybe I was slowly, unconsciously, learning to live in the unseen, uncontrollable flow. All I know is that, looking back, the anger inside had started to feel less vast and volcanic and much more like a small, fluttering bird that fitted perfectly inside my clenched, shaking fist.

I had finally got myself through the worst of it, I felt sure. But the stories that we tell ourselves are often the most untrue. In truth, the longer I lived away from Ireland the more I knew I needed to find my way back. I was, even though I thought I was getting better, becoming less and less able to cope with ordinary life, and I knew, if I am honest, that I really needed help. I needed to let go of the things I had been carrying – heavy, heavy things. There were thoughts churning around inside my head that I knew no one really deserved to have to contend with. I needed to reclaim the words. I needed to break the silence. I needed to go back across all of those borders of the past and displace them one by one, to undo the fear, to write that new language. I needed to befriend that coal-black crow I had met decades before. In short, I needed to resurface and return to reclaim my homeland and my memories for my own.

One Friday evening, five years into living in Edinburgh, a couple of hours after I had arrived home from work, my flat-mate returned to the flat we shared together and found me shaken and weeping uncontrollably, holding my mobile, my bike shoved against the wall in the dark, damp stairwell of our building. She put her coat around me to try to stop me from shivering, and helped me upstairs. I was in too much of a state to talk so she helped me to bed, and I know that she stayed with me until I fell asleep. For many weeks – in different ways, and with different tones – she tried to get me to talk to her about what had happened on that day. She wanted to know what I had heard in whatever call or text she thought must have tipped me over the edge. She wanted to know what bad news I'd received, what had worried me, who had upset me so much. It was such a hard and awkward thing to have to tell her, a friend I love and trust – over and over – that I had absolutely no idea. That I had no clue at all what it was that had brought those tears on, or what – or who – they were for.

I know that it was on that day I received the text message that told me Seamus Heaney, my favourite writer, had died. I do also know that it was only a fortnight after my grandfather had died, too. I know that that particular summer felt like another period of vast, unsettling loss. I know that the more time marched on in my life, the more I felt alone and increasingly unwilling – unable – to take any more. Something important had gone from inside me, I felt sure of that; something vital had been lost along the way. Maybe not on that afternoon in that Edinburgh tenement building, maybe not on the day my bedroom filled with smoke, maybe not on any one day in particular but I felt as if the thing that I had lost was something that, if I wanted to keep living, I needed to get back. Suddenly, the banks were broken and nothing, nothing whatsoever, could hold the river back.

I cried and cried, I wept like a baby, uncontrollably, without having any clue what part of it all the tears were even for. I

wept for days. I cried so much that I had to phone in sick for
the very first time in my working life – not because of flu, or
a broken wrist, but because of grief. When my boss asked me
who had died I was left unable to really find the words. I
wished, I wished so very hard then, that I could find the way
to start. I wished that I could find a way to start to put the
grief into order, to pinpoint the start line, to choose the part
where it would end. I was crying for the years of unwanted
transience. I was crying for my own unbroken silence. I was
crying for lost things, for things not yet lost but that I felt sure
were not going to stay for much longer. I was crying for me,
for so many others; I was crying for the past – for things and
places – for memories, and for things that were never going
to be.

I kept thinking about my grandfather, and his childhood.
By his bed he had always kept the most striking photograph
of his mother. She is almost warrior-like in that picture, gazing
past the camera towards a place unknown. Piercing eyes, a long
neck – taut, like a swan's – an air of the otherworldly in her
stance. I both loved and hated that image, that woman. Her
ancestral draw was so extreme that it called to me, siren-like,
even through the cheap and flimsy paper that could never dare
to capture her on its surface. There is a restlessness to her hands,
a hunger in the way she holds herself. Despite the black and
white of the print, there is no sense of her being in the shadows.
After he died I printed a copy of that picture of my grandfather's mother and put it up in the bathroom of my flat. A
desire came over me to be able to see her when I wanted to,

to nurture an odd sense of intimacy with the image of her – with her ghost, I suppose. To be in some form of communion with the woman who I felt had so utterly failed the man I loved more than any other by abandoning him at such a young age, by leaving him to cope in this world almost completely on his own. It was *her* I wanted to see after he died, not her son. It was *her* that his death helped me to make peace with: that shade of a woman I had never met, one whom I had felt anger towards for decades. Abandonment, like loss, is an odd thing to unravel. It stands on shaky ground. It has thin roots. Those roots are remarkably long, and they are see-through; the damage they do is utterly invisible.

In the last January I spent in Edinburgh, a handful of months after he died, I used the money my grandfather left me to go to Iceland. I was thirty, only just, and I had lost the man I held as my rock in stormy times. I was living a life that looked nothing like how I always thought it would, how I so much wanted it to look. I was drinking every single evening. I was drinking alone. I was drinking to try to forget, to pretend, to mask; I was drinking to try to silence the things that kept creaking and clawing at me like a wild thing trying to get out. When he had died months earlier, I'd known within days what I would do, where I would go to try to grieve him. So I journeyed, in the snow and sleet, in rain that blinded and cut, through as much of the island as I could access. I was trying to find another way to deal with trauma: one that looked different from how it always had before. The most vivid memory I have is of a day spent in Vik – a secluded village, on a beach that is as black as soot. It is the most intense memory of the trip – spent entirely outdoors, in the misty depths of winter.

It was early January. Everything was grey, wolf-howling and grief-laden. My grandfather's face filled my mind, his words danced above the tall, untethered waves just beyond. I remember wondering if the place could sense my sorrow, wondering if my grief could reach the bleak black basalt of the farthest rocks, in fading view. I gathered pebbles, their wet exterior shocked my fingers every time. The caves around the bay seemed like they were gathering something, too. They scooped up the winds, held them in their hollowed interiors until they decided the time had come to spit them back out into the world. The winds taken captive by the caves moaned and called. They sounded like they were answering the skuas and the Arctic terns, the fulmars and the kittiwakes. I remember standing there, curling my shoulders in around my shivering body, thinking about keening – that old, near-lost way of making grief audible, not quite visible but able to be heard. There was no one else around me, the other travellers were in the tea-room, and I threw myself into a fierce gust of wind. The moment shifted and turned, there on that northerly black beach. The light felt weightless. Things that had been so heavy until then lifted, and a soft, untouchable moment came – time held somewhere in-between. *I felt held in a place other than where I was.*

I wailed and shook. It felt like I was standing in a place that I had been before. I imagined my grandfather was there by my freezing, hurting side. I keened for him, and honoured the

loss that might still leave room for hope. It felt as if I was about
to be thrown back into the solid world, but then straight away
I felt like I was drawn in even deeper, held even tighter. I
remember the sense of being in a long, thin tower of light,
and of stillness.

It passed, the light and the stillness, and I found myself
properly back on the soft black sands – even though of course
I hadn't left there at all. I could hear again, then, the sound of
wild birds screeching sharply in the sky. It felt as if they were
lamenting some form of loss, too, on that haunting black stretch
of land.

Grief is sometimes a black bird of sorrow; other times,
though, it is an altogether different creature. Sometimes, when
grief comes, it is full of colours that you have never seen before.
You have to choose what you will do then – if you will stay
with it or not, as it comes in and out of your view. Sometimes,
when grief comes, you must choose if you will run, run, run
– or if you will stay with it, if you will lay your body down,
in time with the chiming of ancient bells.

## CHAPTER NINE

## *Echoing Grief*

WHAT DO WE DO WHEN we name a thing? We carry it from there to here – from then to now – we make room for it in a place deep inside of our being.

What do we do when someone takes away the names of those things that we have named? When we lose the words for what we hold dear? When language splinters and shatters? When the things that mean so much to us become stuck in the bog, so far down that we think that they are gone, so far down that we think that *we* have gone, along with them?

What do we do when we lose the way back to the things we have named?

What do we do when the lights go out in the harbour?

When we lose the harbour itself? What do we do when we lose the way, when we lose our way? When we are caught in the mud and the silt, and we don't know how to come back from the places underneath?

•

When sorrow hit me in Edinburgh, I felt sure I needed to move. I convinced myself the right place was waiting for me – a safe place I could finally call home.

I moved to Bristol to teach in another Steiner school, something I had never really wanted to do in the first place. It was the 'safe' option – one that eased the fear a little, of being in my thirties with no stability, incapable of forming lasting relationships, and unable to stay in one place long enough to make any real go of a life. Teaching allowed me to bury my head in the sand – through the high demands placed on me I had neither time nor energy to even think about dealing with my past. Teaching made me feel as if it was okay to not really be me. Bristol, much as I might have tricked myself into thinking it the turning point of my life, was, just like every other place I'd run to, merely another murky coordinate on the map. Looking back, though, I see that in spite of the confusion and sorrow that still filled my days, the road was widening, even back then. The path was still just as muddy, but I had begun to find a way through. I was not yet upright but I was no longer down on my knees.

I'd been there just over a week when I started my new job. The first day, I came home and headed straight into the garden – full of piercing sunlight reflected off the coat of an urban fox that was curled up on the tin shed's roof. I was reading a book called *Grief Is the Thing with Feathers*, and was finding such resonance in it. The fact that there could be *other* crows, belonging to *other* people, made me feel like maybe I could talk a little about *my* crow out loud. I had begun in those early days in Bristol to really think about grief. And I had stopped batting the thoughts away when they came.

About how grief does not speak the same language as our everyday existence.

How grief is not linear; how it is not even circular. How it grows and mutates, shape-shifts and hides. I still don't know if there is anywhere for grief to go; I still don't know if it ever does go away.

On how grief is not always, though it is sometimes, coal-black as a crow.

How grief is more the moth than the butterfly. Of how moths, in their own way, grieve also. How grief is not always found in the dark – how it might live in bright places, too.

How moths are so unbearably beautiful – achingly so, in fact.

I had begun – tentatively – in Bristol to see a future version of me that might not always be so weighed down. I still mostly felt worthless and heavy. I still felt it might be easier not to be here at all. But there was something that had not been there ever before. For the very first time, there was a hint of *something* right underneath the surface – of something silent and still – something *good*. It would take me years, still, to name it.

·

I was sitting on the back doorstep, in the full glow of the white-yellow sun, reading that book with its crow and its grief, and wondering what we are all to do with all of the sorrow, with the loss that curls up beside so many of us. My mobile beeped on the table in the kitchen behind me, despite the fact that there was no signal to be had in the downstairs of any flat on that entire street. I left the book and got up to check my mobile. The next part happened so quickly that I have never – to this day – properly been able to process it all. The next thing I knew, a sound came unlike any I had ever heard before. It was the sound of glass shattering into hundreds of small pieces, of things being broken that could never be joined to one another again. And, mixed in, there was the sound of a man screaming – the one who was reno-vating the upstairs flat, the flat whose rotted window-frame had just fallen onto the still warm back doorstep of my new home, the spot in which I'd been sitting less than a minute before. That sound of screaming, like an animal, above and all around me. The sound of someone who was sure he had killed the new girl downstairs. He hadn't though, we ascer-tained together when he arrived banging at the front door, in convulsions of hysterical weeping. It was the first time he'd cried since his mother had died a fortnight previously, he told me through his sobs. It was her old home he was gutting, just above my new one. We stood together in a hot pink Bristol kitchen – one I had yet to even cook in. We stood quietly taking in the scene before our grateful eyes. The book I'd been reading before it had happened was still in its place, on the back doorstep. No part of *me* was underneath the debris – the shards of glass and all of the rotted wood. The sound of that glass smashing into hundreds of broken parts, as a grieving grown man cried like a banshee, made me feel like I'd been held upside down and plunged into icy cold water.

I felt parts of me kicking out that I hadn't known were still there. Enough of me was jolted alive – dragged out of the ghost I'd faded into – to know that the time had come to resurface from the Underworld. I could hear the spluttering and choking inside me of someone no longer ready to drown.

I began to drag that not-ghost of myself from place to place, again, just as I had in Scotland, just as I had in Ireland, through the outside world of England and Wales. I cycled along the canal to woods, community farms, hills, quiet hamlets and bustling harbour-sides. I took my slowly, delicately waning sorrow on trains and buses – alongside fields and tracks, rivers and streams, to get off at the sea, the mountains, the chalky cliffs I still dream of. There was no one calling my phone on Sunday evenings any more, to check I'd been outside my flat, so instead I stood outside, alone, on the wet streets of Montpelier – with a bottle of red wine I'd begged myself not to buy wrapped in brown paper by the man at the corner shop with his kind smile. I do not remember a single Sunday evening, no matter how wolf-lunged the weather was, when I didn't walk the length of my street and down the hill to that corner shop to buy the thing that I knew was both numbing and breaking me up. I do not remember a single Sunday evening without standing holding that bottle, delaying letting it enter my eager body as long as I could, under a city sky never quite black enough to feel like night, silently telling the night birds where I had been. Letting the birds of the evening branches, in a tree beside an old church, on a colourful street in inner-city Bristol, take the place of my grandfather on the other end of a phone-line. Sometimes, on such Sunday evenings, my strength felt a little fiercer, more vocal, and I would walk with the brown-papered parcel right past the front door of my flat into the neighbour behind ours – St Paul's. The men who congregated in the square there had moved to Bristol at some or other point along their blood line, some in their own lifetime but many at a point of the line too hazy to see from where they now stood, grey smoke dancing from whatever substance filled their various contraptions and vessels. On those strong Sundays, I would go right up to them, close enough that the beats from their box boomed inside my heart, and I would offer them the unopened wine, 'eeehhhhh' and 'ahhhhhh's, and grateful, jibing laughter being offered to me in return. It seems unreal, and I suppose a little unbelievable, as many true things are – but every single time, no matter which of the four of my seasons in Bristol, when I gave that wine away, I shared the laneway back to my flat with a wild creature. Once it was a jay calling to the branches above him like a mother scolding her babe. Another night it was a tree full of long-tailed tits; twice it was pied wagtails making a shadow-show on the once-white wall beside the house, with its wild pink poppies peeking out through concrete cracks. Too many times to count, though, it was a red fox – as urban as the one I had known before was wild. A silent fox – blood-red, unbidden.

There were so many foxes in Bristol that I began to dream myself as one.

Here I am, trailing my way – hushed and secretive – through darkness that shrouds the city, making a yowling widow's cloak of Leigh Woods. Now I am tearing through allotments – higher, faster, faster, higher – rummaging my way through compost heaps, scraps and peelings silencing the baying my brazen-furred belly fires up to the full moon. Now you see me drinking the River Avon dry – my beast-tongue lapping and licking, slurping and dripping; the water is not water now, you see. I am a wild fox, and I am drinking scarlet-red liquid: blood and wine are my creaturely hydration in these dreams.

Now I am a human again, a woman, and I am thinking of a real night – nearing the midway point of the only autumn I spent in Bristol. It is a planet-bright night, still and shushed. Starlings wheel and cry in the sky above the harbour, a miniature but mighty murmuration. I do not need the coat that I am wearing, and I cannot properly walk in the clogs that I am edging along in towards Colston Hall to meet a new friend and listen to old music: Joanna Newsom, singing songs that have punctuated my sadness for years, with their notes as high-pitched and rare as I imagine those of an albatross to be. I have already downed a bottle of wine, and during the gig I drink furiously, ferociously, like the fox that I have seen myself as in the wine-dark nights. A guy I have been seeing for the last while is there, a few seats behind us, and afterwards he asks

me to go for a drink at a pub called the Christmas Steps. My
friend lives just down the hill, at the harbour, and she wants
to get back to her warm boat, her warm bed, her warm man.
I trot off with this man, this typographer, this man who is as
cold as all of the ones I ever seem to draw towards me, like a
reflection in a frosted mirror. At the pub, I drink and drink
and drink, and a moment comes when I am in the toilet,
having thrown up most of the crimson sea I have downed,
feeling the pull of the river that I know is within spitting
distance of this mirror I cannot will myself to look at. Back
down to the typographer, who does not bat an eyelid when I
tell him I am going – face red from vomiting, salt-streaked like
the barren shores of Donegal, and just as wild. I run, then, in
wooden shoes that I can barely even walk in, knowing I must
drag myself away from the harbour before the water's hungry
call mingles with the fluid in the porcelain-white corridor of
my ear.

I reach the streets of Montpelier before I realise I am being
followed. I cross the street, I slow down, I speed up, I cross
back over again. At the part where I take my phone from my
bag as if to text, he coughs up a hearty, sarcastic laugh. We
both know there is no signal here for at least as many streets
as I can count on the fingers my phone is cradled in. I remember
the latch on my door, how stiff it's been all week, how hard
it's been to unlock. I remember how tightly buckled these
clogs are to try to help me to walk, how hard they would be
to kick off, to give me even half a chance to flee the man
who I now see is stroking silver in his right palm like a blade

of grass. I think of how timely it all feels: the first moment when I have actually run from the desire to end my own life, I end up within arm's length of someone who looks like he might want to end it for me. When the sound comes – piercing and ghostly, arriving from somewhere increasingly close, vibrating around the Bristol street – it lasts the whole way through his looking at me as though it is me making the sound. It lasts the whole way through him booting up the hill in front of us like a startled beast. It lasts the whole way until I see them both – the creatures that are making the sound – two urban foxes in their vicious dance before mating. Their noise only stops when I startle them, sending them into the scrub of the laneway between two abandoned houses, shaken out of their shared moment by the sound of wooden shoes on top of grey concrete.

•

Not quite a year into living in Bristol, nursing yet another hangover and a terrifying sense of breaking point, I took myself on my own to Cornwall for the very first time.

I stayed in an old, tall hostel in St Ives. The light had trickled out nearly completely from a purple-grey sky full of gulls that called to each other, and which turned in the space as if on ropes, on that first night in Cornwall. The winds held a storm inside them. I remember sun that bled out from above the trees and the rooftops, and left a stain across the night's lines; the moment was one of something being halved, and halved again. Then, the wind died down – almost utterly – leaving no trace behind. The magpies on the roof of the cinema across from my room sensed something that should not be there – a creaturely otherness, unbidden, unwelcome – and they made it known.

I awoke after a night full of haunting thoughts – a form of reckoning I had not been expecting at all – and every single image that flooded into my mind was of Ireland. I spent the rest of the day feeling increasingly out of kilter – out of step with all the selves inside me – until I finally accepted I was allowed to feel that way, that it was okay to listen to the sorrow as it reached the highest point, to stand close by as it charted its path back down in small, concentric circles, like a skylark. Even when life – on paper – seems as though all is well, or more than well, the ghosts inside us still sing their hauntings, drag us back to places in our mind: ones we hoped we'd long forgotten.

Over the days that followed, I felt increasingly called back to Ireland. So I followed the beat of the sea and immersed myself in the achingly ethereal Cornish landscape instead, trying to forget the way the light there reminded me of the light in places in Ireland. I spent time in places that – despite the throngs of holiday-makers that had settled in on Cornwall – held no other humans at all. I walked through graveyards, beneath and along cliffs, in coves, beside ruins and stones, relics and strands, underneath skies that held so much more than they could ever dare to share. I swam more than I have ever swum before.

It was beautiful there in St Ives for the entire time – so blue and golden, so full of the sense of time and its unfurling; there was a gentleness to the earth as she spun. The sounds of the busy pathways – crowded, baked – felt muted, as though none of us were quite there. I wandered from place to place as though pulled by an invisible thread – gently but with intent – unsure of myself, of what I was supposed to do. Of how I was supposed to be.

On the beaches, I shared the water with other people almost every time, but in the harbour I swam alone. I could have been a ghost of a soul; I could have been a shadow. It was not the harbour from that night in Bristol, back in the autumn, as a red fox crossed my path for a second time, just like it had when I was wee. But something echoed back to me on that trip to Cornwall from both of those days, from both of those foxes.

I began, slowly, and with a sense of certainty that has not left me since, to feel different. The person I had been for decades was no longer the only one there, in that dawn-bright corner of Cornwall. There was someone else there, too. There was someone else there, nestled inside the body I dragged into the Cornish water. There was another me, inside that body. That body that had dragged itself into other bodies of water in the past. Bodies of water that were colder, darker and deeper than anything I experienced in Cornwall. Bodies of water that, if I had succeeded, I would never have come back out from. Bodies of water that I tried to drown my own body beneath. I realised back then, in the quietness of a hidden Cornish bay, that it was the first time I had ever counted them, those bodies of water I had tried to disappear beneath completely. I realised that it was the first time I had ever sat, alone by the water, and felt glad that my body was still mine, that I had never taken my own life, that my body was still there. That *I* was still there.

•

I swam every chance I got during that time in Cornwall. On the last day, I came out from the water when hunger got the better of me, and walked the grounds of the Irish saint Ia. Ia's story is quite something. She went on the day of sailing to the seashore of her home to depart for Cornwall from her native Ireland along with other saints. Finding that they had gone without her, fearing that she was too young for such a hazardous journey, she was grief-stricken and began to pray. As she prayed, she noticed a small leaf floating on the water and watched it grow bigger and bigger to accommodate her form. She bravely embarked upon the leaf and was carried across the Irish Sea to make her new life in the land of Kernow. Her feast day is 3 February, a handful of days after St Brigid's. Abandonment, being left behind, the need for bravery – the silken balance between delicacy and strength – all these tropes were written into our story long ago as Irish women: the sense of loss, and its ripples, too.

We have been forced into silence, over and over and over again. We have been made to feel unclean, unworthy; we have been made to feel like we are not even really here. We have been beaten and abused, guilted and terrified; we have had the parts of us that are ours, and ours alone, ripped out from inside us, like a page of a story deemed unworthy of being given voice. We have had to keep on, and on, and on. We are women. We are the women of Ireland, and we are breaking the centuries of silence. We are giving wings to the birds in our goddess-born, warrior-strong bodies; these birds are ready to fly.

Oystercatchers made a line out of their flight, as the light made an end to that final day, and I thought of St Brigid, another border-born female – one that we find in the year's darkest days.

When winter lays its head down, memories dance like moths, the delicate ghosts of who we once were. There is a moment – a turning point in our Celtic year – when the Cailleach, the goddess of winter, gives up her crown to let the goddess of spring take her place. The goddess that leads us from that darkness into the golden, healing light is Brigid. Her roots are entwined with an older, pagan goddess, whose festival at Imbolc welcomed the return of lighter days after the darkness of winter. In the Celtic calendar, St Brigid's day falls midway between the winter solstice and vernal equinox and is celebrated on 1 February. It is a moment in the circle of our year when we can see the light reflecting and refracting, when we breathe out the hardship of the winter to learn that we have been strengthened; we have grown.

Brigid was known for her kindness and compassion: a flame

of inspiration in an ancient world of suffering. Once she was milking her mother's cow when a poor woman came by looking for food. Brigid gave her all the milk she had in her bucket. Then she started to milk the cow again, filling another bucket, and again giving it all away to a poor man who came by. The cow had no more milk and Brigid was terrified. The cow rewarded her goodness with more milk.

Born on the threshold of a door at the breaking of dawn, Brigid is a figure of liminality: the human equivalent of a thin place, in many ways. Patron saint of babies and blacksmiths, dairy-maids and fugitives, boatmen – seafarers in general – poets, the poor and many more besides, she represents those voices that for centuries have been silenced. She saw the darkness of the old ways and shone a light on them, showing strength, resilience and that unnamable thing that flows through the blood of a woman. What is it, that thing? What is that thing that makes us women? What is that thing that delivers strength in times of need, that lifts us up when we have been knocked, beaten and kicked down? That thing that keeps us standing, even on the darkest of nights, as the winds rattle at the place we thought we might be safe in? That thing that means we still rise, we still rise, we still and we always rise?

We are women.

Borderlines and the crossing over them are a central theme surrounding the woman that was known as Saint Bride, Bridget, Brigid. For most of my life I have viewed myself as being on the outside – sometimes through choice, sometimes, though, kept away by external forces, from spaces and places without my desire or permission. Often this was due to where I came from, because of the fact of being born in the very particular part of the map that I was. Identity, background, history, belonging, self – all so interlinked, and I had no idea how to untangle each of the strands from the other, no clue how to learn to see myself as something other than what I had lived through, and where I had come from. Bridges, boundaries, barriers: the lexicon of St Bride flowed through my veins like a blood-red cliché.

We are women.

Sometimes, though, the only person – the only thing – keeping us on the outside, making us feel like there is no way back into the harbour, is our own self. And sometimes the moment comes where that falls away, and we learn new words; a different path shows itself after the fog lifts. Sometimes, we even start to see a way through, a way to slip though the borderline: the one we built with our own hands alone.

We are women.

I didn't know a word of Irish back then, not one solitary thing did I know how to offer up, like bird-song, to that hope-bright Cornish sky, but I knew that I would, one day, somehow. That I would learn the words for things I'd spent decades unable to name. When that time comes, I will learn, first, that the Irish for 'to hope' is *dóigh*. I will clasp this knowledge close to my heart, on another day than that one, back on the rugged coast of Cornwall, paying my respect to one Irish woman, and envisioning another.

On another day, many years down the line from that Cornish

one, in another Celtic land, under another sky entirely, I will learn that the Irish for 'to hope' is, too, the Irish for 'to burn'. Embers, holding on for dear life, held tight inside the hearth's womb, waiting to be rekindled. The kindling of yesterday, the women of yesteryear, lighting the flame inside our bellies, feeding the fire inside our hearts on a day not too far away from this one.

•

I made the decision to move back to Ireland from Bristol without any real reasoning or thought process. I handed my notice in, told my flatmate I was leaving and packed up the small amount of possessions I had become used to moving from place to place on the day after I returned from Cornwall. Something had begun to creep through the borderline I had built beneath my skin. Something had begun to eat at it, to work at the gnarly knots; something had begun to break the parts of it up and toss them into the mouth of the hungry sea. Something had started to catch, to burn, to flame. Something had started to hurtle towards me, like a storm.

I already knew exactly what place that storm was going to carry me to.

I already knew exactly what I needed to do.

On the morning of my last day, making ready to leave Bristol and move back home to Derry – something I had sworn I would never, ever do – I stood outside the bit of garden at the front of the house I was in the process of moving out of.

Out of the corner of my eye, movement, the darting of life and colour – a glistening, glimmering dragonfly. It passed so close that I could make out the fine markings on its body, I could see every bit of it, every bit of it there is for us to see. It left the bright, colourful Bristol scene . . . then, less than three minutes later, it returned – it had more to reveal to me – more, still, to remind me of.

The first time I saw a dragonfly, my brother, our mum and I were driving a back-road from Dunree Head to Buncrana, beside squelch-thick, deepest dark bog-land. We'd been on the beach all day – swimming in and out of the shadow as the strong sun blazed. We had watched waves crash against rocks that curved over and back upon themselves, like the arc of a solid blue-grey rainbow. We had let the sun make dimpled patterns on our skin – minuscule islets, where sand had stuck with sweat and sun-cream; a dot-to-dot of tan lines on the map our bodies made of themselves.

Fort Dunree, *Dun Fhraoigh* in Irish, means 'Fort of the Heather' – a reminder that this site has been an important defensive site for Lough Swilly down through history. It has been attacked many times over the years by invaders trying to get a foothold in Ireland including the Vikings, the Normans, the English, the Germans and the French. In 1798 Wolfe Tone was intercepted by the English navy on a French vessel nearby which spurred the British into building Martello fortifications along the Irish and English coastlines.

We had not once thought of any of this past violence, that ghost-trace history, as we swam and ate our sandwiches, as we played 'Pairs' sprawled out on damp towels, as we read until our eyes made blue dots of the yellow-white light, as we drank so many Five Alive cartons that we started to feel a wee bit sick. We were there, in that place, in hiding for the day. We had escaped from a violence much more current, in the fast-beating heart of the city of Derry, than any that the fort may have witnessed in its stone-cold lifetime.

Most of a dragonfly's life is spent as a nymph, beneath the water's surface.

There is, in their ways of acting – of being – a sense of almost hushed secrecy. The sense that they are, in fact, not quite *here* at all. In almost every part of the world dragonflies symbolise change – a form of metamorphosis almost whispered of in their markings.

All of a sudden, just as the dragonfly had drifted into the scene in Bristol, sound filled the air with its energy. A group of lads made their way past me, up from St Paul's, up the hill at Montpelier; they were headed with their sound system to Stokes Croft. They passed me, just once – unlike the dragonfly – but as they did they were close enough for me to see the colours all over their bright, baggy clothes, not quite iridescent – not glistening at all, in fact – but as colourful as that drag-onfly that sent me on my way from Bristol back home to my green island, bodies as full of that darting, indescribable vitality.

There are places that dance on the caves of our insides, even as we try to cover them up from view. We forget their names. We lose their locations on any map. Their coordinates shape-shift and turn themselves into a thing of invisible particles, into a thing not unlike the mist that lives on the frayed and jagged edges of the Atlantic Ocean. Some seem to call us back to them again and again. Some places seem to ring bells, in the dead of night, in those glassy moments of borderless existence, the chiming of which only *we* can hear.

## CHAPTER TEN

## *The Grove of Oaks*

THERE ARE PLACES THAT HAUNT us, from the very first moment we wash up on their shores, well past the point we bid them farewell. There are places that echo on our cavernous insides, long after we make for less ghost-riddled lands. There are places that catch on our hidden parts. We waken from troubled slumber to find them dancing on the walls, shadow-like and spectral. There are places that speak so fully of our loss – of all that we once held dear – that we must shed them, all at once – like the skin from washed-up wood, decaying reminders of all that went before. There are places in the waking world that haunt us even deeper. There are places that we wish to forget for the rest of time but that are part of us, somehow, their barren, salty pathways form the lines of our insides.

•

I left my life in Bristol for my new life in Ireland in the same way I'd arrived – on a ferry that crossed the Irish Sea. Circles

– the closing of them, the completion of cycles and of all the meaning embedded in between – are of vast and unwavering meaning to me, and so it seemed very important to make my return passage to Ireland in exactly the same way as I made my arrival. To make my way across the same roads on the same buses, on the same railway tracks in the same trains, on the same vessels traversing the same seas. It was not lost on me, even back then, that it was still very much the same *me* that navigated this immeasurable and daunting unknown.

I stopped off on the way in west Wales to mark the ending of my old life away from Ireland. I swam at Mwnt – a sheltered cove – in the part of the water where I'd watched dolphins play the year before on my way to settle in Bristol. There were none around on that spring day as the sun hid behind the cliff edge, as the evening reached the sea and filled it with silence. Above me on the land above the bay stood the Church of the Holy Cross, a basic and beautiful wee medieval sailors' Chapel of Ease. It was so calm up there, as calm as it was down below in the water.

A chilly breeze touched the waves, and I remember thinking I was ready to leave the water. But time must have passed without me noticing because the moon was hanging against a darkening blue sky that evening at Mwnt before I left the sea's soothing belly. I don't know how long had passed since I'd told myself that I was getting out.

Gulls had cried above me, the sea had seemed like it was holding its breath. Time hadn't really felt how it normally does that spring evening. There was a moment where I knew the veil had slipped away.

*Honesty, loss, grief, seals, ship-songs, tendons, blood and bone.*

The thoughts that I recall having that night were not even thoughts at all, they weren't as solid as that; the words that flooded my insides were a recollection.

*Hope, breath, memory, place, moths, circles, shadows and light.*

I saw myself as an object on the horizon. I saw myself as I never had before.

*Here, acceptance, always, traces, lines, moons, then and now.*

A wave came, and I knew it was time to leave.

*The veil settled back into its sacred, safe place, and I made for shore.*

I made for land, for the bed I would sleep in for the last night, before crossing the sea back to Ireland.

From that crossing, I remember the light above Holyhead Port, in the tenderly falling spring evening. How it seemed to bleed out over all the soft grey clouds, and the screeching off-white gulls, as they turned in a not-quite-empty sky. The winds – bitter, full of fragments of ice that never quite became earth-bound. The waves – choppy, heaving themselves against the well-faded paintwork of the vessel's iron.

I remember the fear that churned in my belly during that journey 'home', back to Ireland, the land I'd been desperately trying to forget. The crippling anxiety that choked me when I tried to feel positive, when I tried to convince myself that this was the end to the line of sorrow I now knew I could not simply outrun.

Memories re-emerged like the slick black heads of cormorants in the waves, slippery and fleeting. I remember cursing myself for imagining that moving back would somehow fix it all, fix me. I remember standing as the sun tried to break through heavy white clouds and feeling like I was making the biggest mistake in a line of many.

I remember shadows.

I remember darkness.

I remember a coal-black crow watching me as I drank the wine I had brought with me onboard.

I fell asleep on the vessel, in the gap before the black night gave up its delicate ghosts. I saw myself on the hungry river of my hometown, the place I am journeying to.

In the dream I was on a coffin ship. I was wearing tattered brown rags. I was dressed in the dirtied peasant clothes of my ancestors. The night was darker than soot, blacker than a field of ravenous crows trying to dig up the remnants of the crops that didn't come. The night was painted, tar-like with emptiness; loss seeped down from my very bones, through a garment that held no hope of keeping out the cold. I was on a ship, not quite visible beneath the black sky, hidden under smog and freezing fog but still, despite it all, I knew where I was. I knew I was in a time long gone, a time I never witnessed with my own eyes.

I was utterly alone, and was the smallest and the last one to be let on the ship. I was weeping so hard that I couldn't walk in a straight line – my bony shoulders bashed against the wet iron, the metal of the vessel seemed sure to break me. And then the dream shape-shifted and the quay, which had been the departure point, became the destination. We were in Liverpool. We were in India. We were at the most north-westerly tip of Mull. We were in the whiteness at the bottom of Iceland. We were less than a mile further up the river from whence we left. The ship was being thrown around in the blackness by waves sent from an unknown place. We were told to jump – into the blackness, into the unknown, into the belly of the darkness.

I could feel the fear ripping my insides out and firing them up to the starless sky. I could trace my body's borderlines; I could see the death of me coming to meet the life of me on that river. I woke from the dream as we made for land.

I cannot remember the long walk from Dublin Port to the bus depot in the dark, snow-sludged hours before the morning – too early for buses, too shaken to want to take a taxi. I cannot remember the landmarks, nor any sense of fear or upset at arriving over a day later than we were due to because of the storm. I cannot remember what I ate at the port in Wales or how I spent the long, cold, delayed hours. I cannot remember if I realised then or not that something in me had broken so drastically that I was very lucky I had managed that journey across the sea at all.

I cannot remember paying for the bus ticket to Derry. I cannot remember if the driver was male or female, if the radio was on or not, if the snow was still falling on the bus that brought me from Dublin to Derry, the first bus to drive that route on Easter Saturday in 2015.

I cannot remember if I even clocked it at the time, but because of the storm that had howled across the Atlantic, right as I left one life to start a new one, the first morning I would waken in Derry would be the day of the year I found hardest of all. I first ran from an unsafe home as a toddler on an Easter Sunday more than three decades before the one on which I moved back to Derry. I now can't remember what they called that Easter storm of four years ago, if it even had a name at all.

I remember trying to pretend it wasn't Easter Sunday. Covering my ears in the small kitchen of my partner's home in the very heart of the Bogside, as Republican marchers commemorated the Easter Rising, a day almost a century beforehand. We'd only been together – long distance – for three months when I broke down so badly in Bristol that I thought I was going to die. The doctor advised me to think of the person I felt safest around, and allow them to look after me, if they would. M and I had spent time together when I'd been in Derry at Christmas. There was a twenty-two-year age difference, hundreds of miles between where we lived, and he had teenage children who were still a huge part of his life. Still, though, in spite of all the things that made it feel like a badly fated set-up, when I reached rock bottom throughout the rest of that winter in Bristol and into the spring, he was the only person I called. He was the first and only person I'd ever told – at the exact moment of feeling it – that I wanted to take my own life. He did everything within his power to listen, to understand, to help, to stay. Despite the fact that we barely knew one another, the bulk of our communication having been over the phone – each of us in different countries – as soon as I told him I thought moving back to Derry might be essential for my healing, he offered his home as the place I would come to. We didn't talk about how early in our relationship it was, or worry about the state I was in, or the trouble that would be thrown into both of our paths. The moment I arrived off the bus that Easter, he handed me my own key for the door.

In his small galley kitchen – bright green shelves and kitsch deer, vintage Pyrex and black plastic bulls off the end of Spanish wine bottles – a new mug sat alongside all of his much-loved ceramics, bought to welcome me into his fiercely private space. It took years to realise how important the gift of that mug was, both for me and for my relationship with the concept of home.

I remember lying in the bath for the first time in that new terraced house that afternoon and counting back the years as though they were wooden beads on a string. I had been three that Easter Sunday when we ran from my first home – a tall Victorian townhouse in a seaside resort at the end of the train line from here. Twenty-eight years ago, not to the exact date of that Sunday, I'd say, but to the holy day it represented. I would never again set eyes on my maternal grandfather. I would go on, from that day, to run from home after home – often on the very day it was decided I would leave, just like that Easter Sunday. I would force myself, at various points in adulthood, to return to that house, long after the inhabitants I had once known had left. I would stand outside, flooded by the small details that I still remembered: red velvet, the smell of roast beef, my grandfather's hands, grateful that the worse ones – the memories that didn't bear thinking about – seemed to be gone for ever.

M was the only person I felt close to back then. He turned up in my life in the midst of such unthinkable trauma. He is the only person who has done everything he could to keep me safe. When I recall how I treated him in the early days of our relationship I am still almost broken by shame. He was the only one who never hurt me, but he was the only one I fought. I had never, even in my darkest days, retaliated, no matter how badly I'd been treated by others. Here I was, having found someone who treated me with care and love – for the first time in my life – and I was attacking him with every ounce of strength I had inside me. Unbidden, undeserved and without any warning, I pushed and shoved and screamed. I threatened and threw, ridiculed, berated: I abused, I abused, I abused. We had been together less than half a year when I told him that if I took my own life it would be his fault. All that he had done was to love me, and the shock of it left me mirroring many of the disgusting things I had experienced myself – but now *I* was the one carrying out the abuse. I was hurtling towards becoming exactly like so many people I had already started to shed from my life, and the realisation hit me like a body hitting icy water.

There were nights at the beginning of living with M in Derry when I would walk to each of the bridges that span

175

the river, clamber over them and – on two occasions – be dragged away. One night it was by an older lady I had never before seen, on another it was by someone with a face I knew but could not place. I remember the blackness, how high the tidal waters were on each of those nights, how slippery the moss-coated stones, how high the moon-bleached reeds. I cannot remember walking to a variety of different gates in the historic Derry Walls. I do know that I told the person I loved that I was going to jump – in person, in text, on the line of a mobile phone. I cannot remember how much alcohol was involved – so much alcohol, every single day. I don't remember how much I drank. I do remember my partner's face as he wept.

I remember erasing note after note drafted on my phone trying to convince myself there was no point in me still being here. I remember having to continue as normal, as if nothing bad had happened. Derry felt just as it always had in many respects but also like a foreign land. The streets all looked the same, my family set-up felt just how it always had, but I felt like I belonged there even less than I had before despite now having a supportive partner, and a safe place to call home. I was trying to help M run his business, trying to get to know any of the people in and around my age in Derry, but there were very few – almost everyone I knew before had moved away because they had found living there too much of a struggle. Things were hard for M and me for a long time after I moved in, and we had no one we could turn to. Things like trauma, and the impact on a home environment, are difficult topics to broach. I told my mother and father of these things, only once, on separate occasions, crying out for help. It never came. It has never been spoken of by either of them to me since.

When I think back to those first months in Derry I see the silvered reflection of the metal on the old railway track 'out the line', beneath a bright crescent moon, the night my life was at the most risk. I see reeds that I remember from childhood, moss that glows as though it is from another planet; I see birds of the night – hunting and haunting their prey. I remember the fear inside me that things would never change, as I lay in the cold beneath a Brutalist concrete bridge with night lorries speeding over it.

I could not see a way through. A way out. A future. I could not think of a way to keep myself away from that river. How I might ever keep my head above water. I did not yet know that there is none of it, not one single, solitary part, that is my fault. I could not see, back then, that I did not deserve those things that happened. That the way I felt would, one day, leave me. That it may still resurface, at times of darkness, but that I might have found safe passage.

I imagined, in moments of panic and confusion, growing old alone. I imagined the broken family I come from becoming ever more distant. I imagined M throwing me out, and I wonder now if I was actually trying to push him into doing it, in some twisted form of further self-harm.

I could not imagine a way through it all. I could not imagine a future. I could not imagine that I would ever learn to talk about things that I went through, that I was made to keep silent about for decades. Most of all, back then, I could not imagine healing.

I could not imagine there ever being a Sunday morning, sober and full of gratitude, where I would watch birds lift up from a yew tree into the waiting arms of the winter storm.

I could not imagine the future that still lay in wait for me, like a soft seed.

I could not imagine light, so much light – light like a flock of white birds in a winter sky.

●

When I returned there, to that city of oaks, built on the banks of the River Foyle, just as I had when I'd moved to every other place I'd run to, I thought it was for good. The details of the first few years, all the ins and outs that came together to make an image, like an old photograph, fade into the grey of memory. There was unrivalled, harrowing trauma coming back to me day in and day out. It came from the very beginning, as though the lid of a pot had been lifted off, and every single ounce of fluid was evaporating before my eyes. Like a river that had burst its banks. Like ice beginning to thaw. I was utterly out of control, out of my depth, and I had no idea where to turn. Nightmares, fevers, panic attacks – all things I knew well from previous episodes of life, but now they were a different shape. The triggers that had once been few and far between now surrounded me at all angles. When M told me in the summer that there hadn't been a single week since I'd moved back that I hadn't spoken of taking my own life, he begged me to make an appointment to speak to the doctor. I was seen immediately. The GP told me that I should have seen someone long, long back. That I should have been signed off work in Bristol – that I should maybe even have had a proper break from work as far back as Edinburgh. He looked at the record in front of him, listened to only the briefest of outlines of the life I'd lived, and said that I should feel very proud of how I'd managed to get through. He told me – the very first time I had ever heard the words come from anyone's mouth – that I did not deserve to feel the way I felt any longer. I didn't weep in his room. I didn't shake. I was too numb to even speak.

I had finally told someone about things that had happened to me but that I had grown used to leaving out. I told him how even thinking about trying to talk of these things to my family – people who know almost all of it, people who also went through it – makes me want to kill myself. I told him that I cannot undo any of the thick knots. I told him that I am drinking myself to death. That I am wandering barefoot in my nightie in the Bogside, out at the old abandoned railway line, through the marshes that are the marker between the land and the river. I told him that I don't know who I am underneath it all, that I am worried I'm becoming the same as people who have hurt me so deeply. I told the doctor, on that bright day in June 2016, that I was scared, so scared, and that I needed to make it all stop. He placed me on the priority list for therapy and counselling. He found me a way to talk about the various forms of abuse that I had carried for decades, the trauma I had dragged from place to place for my entire life. I started therapy that summer, a handful of months after returning to Derry, and I stayed in therapy for a full year.

During that year, the suicidal thoughts did not go away completely. They did not ease much at all, in fact. The drinking every day and wandering the streets at all hours of the morning did not stop. I continued to walk out of my new home feeling certain that it was for the very last time. I still found myself at the river during that year. But something was different; something was changing. Through therapy – the hardest thing I have ever done – I was given a safe place in which to break the silence I had carried for decades. Week in, week out, through the first four seasons I spent in my hometown as an adult, I was told, over and over, by someone I trusted, that I was allowed to feel how I felt. I was allowed to share, without judgement, the way I felt about myself and others – those still here and those now lost. I spoke about pain I'd experienced in relationships with those very close to me – my parents, my wider family, my closest female friend. Every week, without fail, I came away with the feeling that my being here, in this world still, mattered. That keeping me here, in it, was a thing worth time and care.

Every step of the way, no matter how much I lashed out at him, M continued to love and care for me – this person whom he'd known for so short a time, and who had treated him like an enemy for much of it. There is a chance that during that first year in Derry, when I attended therapy and counselling every week, I hit my lowest point, but it's a bit difficult to recall the actual chronology. It could just as easily have been the year that followed, which was almost as harrowing as the first. Trauma does that. It takes the truth and distorts it, it jumbles up the timeline, it hides things away for innumerable days. Alcohol does these things too.

I cannot remember many specific details of my first two years back in Ireland; they all swim together into a sense of a life being formed for the very first time. People came and went, as they always do. Slowly, I lashed out a little less at the person who nurtured and cared for me. I formed a handful of relationships with people I trusted enough to be around but not enough to talk to about my mental health. I started to run again, and I learned to stop when I needed to, instead of pushing my body too hard. M and I found that we worked together incredibly well outside our house, and we put our energy and time into a vegan café and arts space, first in an old shirt factory, then in a building built into the historic Derry Walls. The café was the only place where you could sit with a coffee, reading, writing or simply just being, beside the city's walls. Those walls that once divided that city of oaks, that were the source of such devastating bloodshed and loss. The café was the first building as you left the Bogside and entered through the walls into the city's heart. Something about choosing that particular building as the one we would bring back to life – the one where we would offer free food to those in need, safe places to share writing, performance, and hold meetings about the environment, a space to discuss the earth and the parts we might play in our community – changed me in ways I am still only beginning to understand. Only a few weeks after we opened riots started again. Bombs were being made again, cars were being burned again, police were being targeted again, and the local community organised a vigil. It was held at the top of Fahan Street – the street leading up from the Free Derry Wall, the nucleus of the fighting – right in front of our new business. For almost a week in the run-up to the community meeting, young lads had been jumping off the Derry Walls onto the flat roof of our café and throwing bottles and rocks in their angry, confused rioting. That evening, we stood together, people from both sides of the river, Catholics, Protestants and those of us who are sick of those divisions, and tried to find a way to reach the members of our community who were so full of anger and fear. Who could see no future for themselves in that city, and didn't know any other way to act. I cried my heart out – partly because of fear for what the future held for Derry, but mostly because of the light that had come, all out of nowhere, a light that I had never seen on people's faces before that night. People who years ago might have not only condoned the violence but encouraged it were now standing shoulder to shoulder with people from the other side of the river, emboldened and courageous, ready to fight for a different future – this time with hope, not fear. Something shifted then. I stood tall and hopeful too, fiercely proud of the place I came from, and of all that it had become – of all that it had the potential to grow into, still.

Early into our relationship, just months after I'd moved in, M made a very important decision to start driving again.

He'd been without a vehicle for years at that point following a traumatising experience that left him too scared to get behind the wheel. I don't drive, and public transport in rural Ireland is expensive, infrequent and unreliable. M felt that getting out to the wilds of Ireland was a very important thing for me, for my healing and for our relationship. So we bought an old beat-up green Mercedes. I watched as the man I loved faced his fears with each short trip, building up confidence and rekindling a love of driving he thought was gone for ever, to bring me to places he knew I really needed to be. I could once again bring myself into the safekeeping of the land around me, as I had done everywhere else I'd lived. I let it hold me close. I let it carve out space inside me for healing. We explored every last bit of Donegal – so many wee nooks and hidden coves neither of us had ever seen before, stretches of shoreline as if from another time, hills full of ancient stones and untold stories – over and over the land kept me safe. When our car broke, we bought a van, allowing us to sleep on a mattress in the back at any place we found for the night. Soon we went further, in every direction – north, south, east, west – to places we returned to over and over, and to places that we never once went back to. We found a sheep's skull at the wee beach beneath Fort Dunree one wet, misty January day – nearing the end of my therapy – and both saw it for the gift that it was: a marker of that day. We set off to find a particular harbour I remembered from childhood that never turned up, and in its place we found the most ethereal, misty bay we'd ever seen. There were harrowing days, and haunting days, and days so full of hope and light that I howled like a wolf.

M gave me the space and solitude I needed but often I wanted him to stay – to be there in the places I was craving, too – silently, by my side. It was the first time I'd ever welcomed the company of another person in my space at times of grief and confusion. There was swimming, so much swimming, and there were feathers and stones almost everywhere I looked. There was still pain and trauma, and for some time there was still a deep-rooted addiction and, when it went, a whole new layer of trauma was unearthed. Once those first two years had passed, though, I never tried to give my life over to anything unsafe again. To any place, thing, person or thought that would place me in any real danger. Something shifted, something vast, and it never came back.

In the third year back, on the first of January 2019, at the age of thirty-five, after awakening on my first New Year's Day as a non-drinker, I was heralded into my first swim of the year in the Atlantic Ocean by a curfew of curlew at Shroove Lighthouse. Just past was the first Christmas and the first birthday I have ever had in which I did not shed a single tear. That bird of grief, the one I met in my childhood bedroom, thick with smoke and unimaginable sorrow, did not take his place at my table that December, even though I had made proper room for him this year for the very first time. In that third year back in Derry, I had – silently, without any marking of it – made room to sit with my grief. I had stopped lashing out at M; my angry, violent outbursts had gone away completely, and a year had passed free from any thoughts of suicide for the first time in over a decade. The night before, on New Year's Eve 2018, my dad had sat by my fire, opposite me, the first fire he had ever watched me light with my own hands.

When he arrived I was drawing a wren. We talked about the collective terms for birds. We talked about the coastline of Donegal, of our experiences there – mostly separate from one another – and I told him about a day on which I had been followed by a wild red fox to the cove at Kinnagoe Bay. Midnight came and passed us by, gently and without the sense of any deep undoing or reshaping, leaving no trace of that huge transformation we assume such moments will carry in their wake. When he left, just before one a.m., I realised it was the first New Year of my entire life that I had watched an old year become a new one with my dad.

The next day, as I swam beneath curlews, I thought about the first time I heard the cry of a curlew in the company of another human. It was on Inch Island that first year I moved back, while walking with my dad through tall reeds under a beautiful winter sky filled with starlings. Less than a minute after the curlew broke that December silence, he told me, for the first time, that he had almost drowned when he was eighteen after being caught up in reeds beside a swan's nest. He never explained why he chose *that* particular moment to share such a traumatising part of the story of his life, a life that I knew very little about. To this day I believe that the thing that swept away decades of distance, and which caught my dad so offguard, which made him so honest and brave, was that curlew's cry in the soft, pink December sky. The three of us were held in one of the thinnest places I have ever set foot, in the space in between.

By the time my father and I had reached the water's edge, where our bodies met the outline of the world, where the waves met the land, another borderline had been wiped off the map.

I've spent much time recently trying to place all of my experiences in Derry into some form of a pattern. In truth, though, lots of it feels jumbled and hazy – a reflection of what I lived through there over all the decades that came before. Ghosts and fragments, reflections and mud, and then the unmapped, unknown point of the map – where light began to fill in the gaps left over.

Two years after I moved home, in 2017, in the April after the UK voted to leave the EU, I had a piece of artwork on display in an exhibition entitled *Border* alongside twenty-three other female artists at the Void Gallery in Derry. We first met to begin work on the *Border* project on the first day of February. St Brigid is said to have called wild birds to her hand, and in rough weather she sent them to guide sailors to safety. My favourite St Brigid story is of her teaching the oystercatcher to build his nest above the line that the sea leaves behind in its wake to save his young from the fierce storms of winter. From the meeting room where we sat at that first gathering we could see where Clinton had stood in Guildhall Square, so many moons before. We could see the Peace Bridge, and the striking River Foyle. The following morning, a young lad in his early twenties put himself into that river, gave himself to that body of water we had looked out on and spoken of in such depth the night before – that border between the visible and the invisible. There were rumours that the place he had chosen to go in was in the part where the city becomes a boggy estuary, the part of the river I had been drawn to over and over for the first few years. For the entirety of our project, folk from both sides of that river – Protestant and Catholic, political and apolitical – trudged through deep mud, along dark black tracks, underneath a sky filled with varying stages of a new moon, the first of that spring. The whole of Derry-Doire-Londonderry came out together, side by side, to try to claim back a son that the entire city had lost to the hungry river.

During my research for the *Border* project I was touched by the discovery of the closeness in meaning of the words *mneme* and *neomenia*. The first noun translates as '*the ability to retain a memory of the past experiences, patterns of behaviour or cultural practices or ideas of its own and past generations and to transmit these to future generations*'. (Mneme, from Greek mythology, was the muse of memory.)

*Neomenia* translates as '*the time of the new moon; the beginning of a month in a lunar calendar*'. I began to think about the moon, and the possible effects it might have on us all, and on me as a woman. I thought about the effects it might have on our river, and on our memory, both individual and collective. What effect does living by a body of water have on us? What about the effects of our past? What about when we leave a place, the place where we were born? When it all becomes too much? When the river feels like the only place that might be able to hold all of our grief, our bodies coated with shame? Why are so many of us coming home, now? Is it possible that we are being called back, just when we are needed on this island the most? Just when *we* need the island, ourselves, to make a place inside us to heal.

We hung our work for the *Border* project on 21 March – the first full day of spring in 2017, following the vernal equinox of the previous day. I awoke that day in a room full of soft yellow-grey light, filtering in through white muslin. That morning snow fell thick and fast – grey as fresh ash against that window of my attic room overlooking the Peace Bridge. The news reached me that Martin McGuinness – a man so deeply embedded in the beating and bruised heart of my city – had passed away. I was caught utterly off guard, as gusts of wind blew the white dust all around the rooftops. There is a terrifying violence to the past of my hometown, like those of many others', but in that moment I felt fiercely grateful for the handful of people who chose, finally, to undo their own chains when they did. For the fact that, somehow, after decades of violence, they allowed themselves to meet on the middle ground despite their crow-black past. For the fact that people who had once planted bombs somehow found a way to plant seeds – seeds of peace – side by side in a city begging on its hand and knees for reconciliation. A city desperate for tall, strong, healing oak trees to be allowed to grow in its soil once more.

In between the hanging of our exhibition and its opening night, Martin McGuinness, a man held in contempt by many but who in later life turned his back on his violent past and played an incomparable role in forging a pathway towards peace in the city of Derry, was buried. Snow swirled outside that morning, and M brought me a coffee to drink, looking out over the rooftops of our city. I glanced at that river, the Peace Bridge and Guildhall Square, where I first heard words of peace that stayed with me for ever, and every single bit of it filled me with grateful tears. That afternoon at the funeral, I listened to the words of Bill Clinton once more, this time in a very differently mapped city from the one I had stood in as a terrified eleven-year-old girl, in the square below my window.

At McGuinness's funeral, Clinton spoke of the journey that we as a city and island have come on throughout our Peace Process – one that was navigated through choppy, stormy and uncertain waters. He recounted walking across the Peace Bridge with McGuinness and John Hume – and spoke of what he considered to be McGuinness's utter metamorphosis – from a man of violence to a man of peace.

Clinton once again ended with Heaney:

*Believe me – when the people who made this peace did it, every single one of them decided to take a flying leap into the unknown against their better judgement.*

One hour before we opened our exhibition to the public, a body taken out of the River Foyle was confirmed to be that of the young lad that the city of Derry had searched for together, side by side. Later that morning I watched a solitary heron fly low, directly above the votive candles that had been kept lit throughout the search, on the Protestant side of the Peace Bridge where the young lad came from, by members of the Catholic community from the other side.

When I moved back here, after a decade and a half spent away from the place I was born, there was no way that any of us could have foretold the changes that would land on this city, like a bird shot down from the sky above that vast, deep river. That Brexit vote, in the year that I moved home, felt too surreal to really sink in. Even now, I wonder if I would have done anything differently in that spring of 2016 – if I'd known that all of this would happen. If I'd known that I would watch the city begin to sink back down into thick, dark mud. If I'd known that murder would be back on our lips again, helicopters back in our night skies, mourning back in our hearts, fear back in the pits of our bellies. I wonder what I would have done. I wonder if I would have been brave enough to come back here, to this shifting, turning, cracking city. I wonder if it would have been the same path I would have trodden; I wonder if I would be at this point of the line now, at this point of the circle. Would I have guessed, too, the things I would go through here in those years, the changes that would enter into my life, the peace that I would, somehow, finally feel, in beside my bones?

Those candles were still lit that morning after the young lad's body had been found at the edge-land of the city, given back by the hungry river, their lights flickering in the soft glow of morning in memory of him. I felt a change in the air back then in that city of mine, despite the chaos and uncertainty that Brexit is blowing in on stormy winds. I could hear the beat of something stronger – much, much stronger – in the morning's breeze.

•

There are places that are so thin that we see right through it all, through the untruths we have told ourselves about who we are. We see through every last bit of the things that we once thought defined us. We see that, like a landscape that has undergone vast and irreversible shifts, we, too, might be capable of change.

We see that there might, in fact, be something a little like grace to an object that has been battered and undone, hewn away to less than it once was, chiselled and broken, sculpted and reworked into something so different from its original form.

We see that we, too, might learn to live in a different way – within a changed and changing form. New, whittled lines alongside the old, healed cracks.

## CHAPTER ELEVEN

## *Skull of a Shae*

THE ISLAND ON WHICH I was born is a wild, ancient and stirring place – a place so ethereal as to take a given moment in time and bathe it in the light of something divine, a place that was eternal and holy long before those words ever had need for voicing.

It is a changeable and changing place. You will not leave my island the same person you were when you first found your way to her shores. Ireland is somewhere that burrows deep down, in beside the parts of you built of bone and of marrow, before you even know that you have arrived – before you even embark, perhaps. It has been painted as a lush island – the colour green spilling out of every corner – but those of us who call it home would tell you a different story. Ireland is an island bathed in colours the like of which I can never properly fathom, more than three decades since I arrived on her shores.

She is the yellow of the lichen that covers ancient rocks – set in circles – that protect the surface of hidden and sacred gathering places.

She is the grey – so many greys – that records the passing of days, of years, of millennia, stones that speak of time, and of all that cannot really ever be kept in any one place.

She is blue – a blue that I have never really seen in any other place on earth – each of her bodies of water seems to embody a different shade of blue from the others. The river that flows through my hometown is, betimes, the most flawless blue I have ever set eyes upon – inky, fading into cyan and, in some lights, royal, even delft in others. But that river of mine is also a shape-shifter; it holds too many colours inside its belly to even begin to list. When the autumn settles in along its reed-fringed verges, my river seems as though it is almost the brown of the muck and sediment – as if the silt has made its way up from the unfathomable depths beneath to greet the wind as it rustles through the timeworn oaks above.

Ireland – this ethereal and mythical island, set down in the heart of the ravenous, tumultuous Atlantic Ocean – is black, too, coal-black, as black as to be the making of the crows. Black is the colour of many of our true loves' hairs on this island but it is also the colour of sorrow and fear – of mystery and the unknown, of so much death, and of the unimaginable depths of our grief.

•

I have been back on this island of many colours for three and a half years, now. Here I am, living a stone's throw from the geographical spaces that heaped the most trauma onto my path.

The natural world in the wilderness on both sides of that unseen border dragged me back to the land of the living, and it held me there. In childhood, it was the compass that guided me through an unnavigable body of water created by the Troubles that battered Ireland. In adulthood, it has held me just as tightly, as I dealt with the trauma that had rained down on me for decades, in the wake the Troubles had left behind them. Every bird – goldfinch, whooper swan, oystercatcher, corncrake, white lady peacock, curlew – held the promise of an escape from the present moment, a new path of flight. Every butterfly and moth – tortoiseshell, peacock, cinnabar, copper, speckled wood – spoke of hope and the potential for unrecognisable change. That change so many of us had hoped for came to this island, but now all of the solid, irreplaceable progress made in the last years is at risk of being lost, along with so many other precious things that are under threat in our world right now. It is our duty, all of us, to use our voices, to tell those who are dragging us down into the darkest reaches: *we are not ready for this, enough, already, enough.*

This story, like all stories of all people and places, has more layers than I may ever fully know, than I could even try to peel back, but I am trying. I will always try to understand this story – my story, our story. The violence, bloodshed and trauma that crossed my path within less than a mile of this street I now live on are a part of my past that I can never undo. They are a part of this city's history, this island's, and the world's too; these events speak to – and of – our race.

Much, so much, has been lost; so much that we once held

close here is gone, and that loss is another thing that cannot be undone; those things cannot be hauled back out from the thick tar-dark bog-land of the past. There is, though, underneath the darkening sky – beneath the layer of fear that politics, poverty and anxiety have scarred the moment with – so much to be found; glints of light shine up from the mud, like gold teeth in an old, wise mouth.

Outside, as the months of 2019 have passed by, fierce winds have ripped through this land. The political uncertainty and darkness began, in the last year or so, to feel as though it was actually becoming a visible, fixed layer of the actual landscape of the North itself. On we who were there in that landscape, just trying to stay calm, just trying to find the strength to shout about things like hope. A moment came, at the start of this year, when things felt as if they had reached rock bottom. When I look back over 2019 it is a wee girl that I see, not a grown woman. A wee girl who is terrified that the darkness of the past might come back – of a cruel, ebony crow coming back to hide away all the light.

That crow I met when my home was bombed in the dead of a Derry night held me tightly in his silent grip for decades. At the beginning he was bigger than life itself, holding the optical illusion of the world in his strong beak. For the first time since I moved back to Ireland, there have been days in this dark year, just on its way out, when my crow has had the strongest silhouette in my life so far, when he has had the vastest, blackest wings. There have been days – so many days – this year when I could see the little girl I was way back on that deprived, violent housing estate – and to some extent, still am. I am not ready to go back there; I have worked too hard just to keep myself upright – to keep my eyes looking to the sky, looking for the beat and light of life. I battle – I really try to – the sense of being dragged up, away – I try to ignore the calling away that the sorrow always brings.

Fires rage through the city – death threats and the constant undercurrent of violence are back on the scene once more – petrol bombs are made and thrown from the city's walls. I watch the scorched land try to steady herself; I take notes – I try to drink in her courage, to mirror her resilience. We are a month away from Brexit, now, apparently. The moment of the General Election has arrived. The United Kingdom is far from united; the divisions seem to deepen, to widen, as the days run away as if towards an invisible horizon. The countdown here – at many border-places on the map – has begun to morph into an unimaginable confusion. All the while, the larger world spins – quicker, more uncontrollably, towards the edge.

As has been the way, over and over again in times of sorrow, my darkened mood took me into the landscape, into the belly of the untamed, ever impartial Atlantic Ocean, and into places as thin as winter light, as thin as the mist above the sea. To come from a place where speaking – where the telling of your own story – can be taken out of context, twisted, coiled over upon itself into a serpentine mess, is sometimes a hard thing to bear. Many of us who lived through the Troubles in the north-west of Ireland buried our head in the sand and tried to pretend we were impervious to the things that had seeped down into the parts underneath our skin. We slithered away from our past – from our experiences – like eels.

There are places, though, in which, no matter how much sand you might find in which to try to disappear, you will meet yourself at every given point on the compass; you cannot hide from your own story in certain places on this map of ours. The Troubles in Ireland were, for me, utterly categorised by the loss of safe places. I am not ready to feel unsafe, to feel that there is no place for me to shelter, ever, ever again.

The politics that have played out on the island of Ireland for centuries now have left many of us here a little wary of imagining a safe future. Who are we to vote for? Who will steer *us* through? Where – if there even is one – is our safe harbour? The poverty, fear and trauma hidden in the folds of my small Atlantic rock, its lands to the north, south, east and west, those sharp fault lines of division between my kinfolk: these things are not completely removed from the larger issues on the table, on our planet as a whole. We are losing blackbirds. We have lost fathers, mothers, children, friends, teachers, homes, schools, places of worship, identity, compassion. We are losing our young, though some of them have not died. We are losing our way. We are losing *the way*. We have lost; we are losing. We are, though, still here. The blackbird is still here. There is still so much left here for us to protect, to nurture, to preserve, to hold dear.

Blackbirds symbolise reincarnation in many corners of our world. In Ireland, blackbirds sit in close company with the element of water. Two blackbirds seen together means good luck. They are also regarded as messengers of the dead. In the same vein as the crow and the raven, the blackbird is often considered a bad omen. In Ireland in the nineteenth century, blackbirds were said to hold the souls of those in Purgatory until Judgement Day. It was said that whenever the voices of blackbirds were particularly shrill, it was those waiting souls, parched and burning in the fires, calling out for the rain. The rain always followed. The whistle of the blackbird at dawn warned of rain and mist for the coming day. We have been listening to, and looking at, these birds that we share space with for many moons.

My favourite tale of the blackbird is about St Kevin, an Irish sixth-century saint who was at one with the natural world around him. It is said that in the temple of the rock at Glendalough, St Kevin was praying with his hand outstretched upwards when a blackbird flew down and laid her eggs in his palm. Old words passed down have it that the saint remained still – unmoving and resolute as the earth herself, for as long as it took for the eggs to hatch and the brood to learn slowly how to fly the nest that he held safely within his hands. St Kevin, many centuries ago, may have already been attuned to a concept we view now as an imperative one, one that worries us right into our depths, growing more and more relevant as each day passes: that of 'ecological grief'. St Kevin, like many of us in this age, simply could not allow for any more loss.

We have a somewhat difficult relationship with the word 'tradition' in Ireland, particularly in the North. The way that religion has latched itself onto the politics of this land has left many people with no desire to look at the imagery of their ancestors: the story of their past. We have lost, broken, murdered, burned, stolen, hidden and undone – all in the false name of tradition. Lives, places, and stories have been ripped out by their roots because '*that's how it has always been*'. I wonder, I wonder so very much these days, what wealth of imagery and meaning was lost when we became so focused on our differences here, that we buried the things that had once tied us together, the things that might still know a way through, for us all.

Once, twenty years ago, when I was not quite sixteen, my grandfather and I had a conversation that has stayed with me for almost two decades. My grandfather 'called on people', and I see now how lucky I was to be taken along with him on his trips in and out of various homes and workplaces, greeted many times a day by so many different people from various backgrounds that I lost count. He was drawn to people who looked after those who needed to be cared for. He counted amongst his friends people who rehomed pigeons and canaries, and an old woman whose 'two-up-two-down' house had so many dog baskets that she had to keep her kitchen table folded up beside her ironing board and hope meal times would be dry enough that she could eat on the street outside her front door. My grandfather had friends who worked every hour sent to them volunteering for the Salvation Army, the Churches Trust, St Vincent de Paul, the Men's Mission and more. I never understood until very recently why my grandfather was never happy to be in the house he so dearly loved, in the comfort of his own sitting room. Why, after decades working himself to the bone, did he not just want to slow down and begin to enjoy his time at home, to relax in his own place with his own family? I know what drove my grandfather towards showing the care towards others that he did, now. I think that growing up without a parent – perhaps particularly your mother – as a constant, reliable source of support, protection and love, does something to a person over which they have no real control. It changes you so drastically, so fundamentally, that you have to make a choice: what am I to do with all of this hurt? My grandfather chose to find his own way through it, to stop it from taking root and turning into bitterness and anger. My grandfather found the courage to step out of the cycle. My grandfather took his suffering and he turned it into empathy, into compassion; he gave those around him that which he had never been given.

I remember that day that my gentle, inspiring grandfather and I talked about knowing people as clearly as though it were happening right now, this very moment. It was in October, two decades ago. It was, in fact, on the day of my father's birthday. He was spending it how he always had done since he'd moved out of our house – with his new family, without us. Somehow being on the verge of turning sixteen – hurtling headlong towards adulthood – was what made the loss of him really sink in, despite the fact he had, by that point, already spent many other birthdays away from us. I'm not sure exactly why it affected me so deeply on that particular one, and maybe I never will. That bit doesn't really matter so much now.

I remember telling my grandfather that day that if my father – his son – were to die, I would not attend his funeral. I appreciate that statements such as those – extreme, sweeping, black and white – are normal as a teenager. However, that feeling I voiced to my grandfather that autumn afternoon would end up settling in under my skin. It warped and morphed and left me feeling desolate and empty. It stayed for over a decade – it created a void in a place I could not locate. I felt so angry with my father for leaving and not helping us in ways I thought he should have. I placed the blame for that petrol bomb on his shoulders, childishly. For many years I blamed him, and everyone else around me, for the fact that I never felt safe – for the loss and the grief. For all the grief, for all the grief I could never quite find words for. My grandfather did not show any anger, place any judgement or try to change my mind. Instead, after listening, he placed his soft, cracked hands over mine and asked me if I wanted tea. He made it, and then *he* talked.

He talked about birds. He talked about how once when he was a little boy he'd stood beneath an oak tree while a small bird flitted between its branches. He talked about how the bird was golden, like the earth on fire, with red flames and wee black bits like coal spat back out onto the hearth. How he'd jumped up and down in excitement, convinced they were from another place – blown in on the Atlantic winds, of another world than his. The man he was along with, the next-door neighbour of the two sisters (not relations), who were 'rearing' my grandfather, said: *'Goldfinch, lad. Wait de ye see a charm o' them. Quare brings a smile de yer fis, I'll tell ye that.'*

The next time a single bird ever brought such joy to that wee face of his was almost two decades later. He was in his early twenties then, he told me, and had only just arrived on Canadian shores, fresh off the boat from the port of Derry. His older sister was waiting for him. Zipping about in the air above the port were iridescent birds the like of which my grandfather had never seen before. He had been held in a big ship by the belly of the sea for weeks, unable to sleep or hold food down properly on the journey from his impoverished homeland to this new land of promise, a place full of the future. The birds flew all around his tired head, twittering and chee-cheeing, as though they had come out as his welcome party.

He talked about how they looked – so beautiful – midway between a magpie and one of our own migrant birds. They were dark and metallic with bronze-green upper parts, a violet rump and tail, the latter slightly forked, with white underparts. Like an oil-slick puddle painted onto a showy wee Canadian bird. It was not, strictly speaking, he told me, a Canadian bird. It was a migrant. The birds he was welcomed onto Canadian soil by were violet-green swallows, who had only just arrived on the same shore themselves. The violet-green swallow is one of the first birds to arrive in Canada in springtime, and is amongst the first migrant birds to depart in the summer. Those early spring migrants, like my grandfather had done, tend to follow the coastline as they journey.

The scientific name for the violet-green swallow is *Tachycineta thalassina* – meaning 'fast moving' and 'of the sea' – alluding to the sea-green colour of their backs. My grandfather watched them for less than a week before giving in to the soft, still call of his homeland. My great-aunt told me years after about how her younger brother had woken the travel agent up in the middle of the night, at his home, to make sure he could secure him a place on the first boat heading back to Derry that very morning. Canada was not the place – nor the life – for him, and he left it quicker than even those wee migrant birds. He never saw a violet-green swallow again for all of the decades he lived but he spoke of them to me often, right up until the week he died.

As he prepared to pass over into that unknown place, in his mid nineties, my grandfather named the birds right outside the window with me as he made ready for the next realm. Everyday garden birds, the same ones he had heard for nine decades in that very city, never more than a few miles from that very bed. The whole time, as I held his speckled, paper-thin hands, he asked me to tell him about places, about all the places I had been, about all those places that he hadn't seen.

There are places where there are no boundaries between things, people, places or time, in which all that we once knew can still dance right before our eyes. All that we once held dear and true – all that we once placed such immeasurable value upon – we *can* know again; we can learn to hold those things in deepest respect, once more. In some places there is room for more – for so much more – to find its way onto our grateful, echoing insides. My ancestors believed that to behold the divine, all that was other than our own selves, you needed to be ready. Those who stood in a line too long, too far back for me to see the end-point, believed that place and time came together, in those delicate moments, to meet your own willing self. They believed that they were not alone in that line, neither was that line one that only embraced that which was human. As my grandfather began the process of dying, I dreamed of him on innumerable nights and untold days as a winged creature. I watched him crawl through dirt and grasses, searching for food. I watched him lift up from broken, fallen branches. I watched him soar and hunt and circle. And in only one dream I watched him sleep, above a golden, empty desert, on the wing.

I think so much in these troubled, dividing days, about what it might mean to live as the birds do, as the moths and butter-flies, as we once did ourselves maybe: free from border and barrier – in a place where the veil is so thin that we are reminded what it means to really *be here* – in this glorious world.

Place is a whistling, slippery eel, too, though, and it has haunted us here on this island for centuries. It is so intimately linked with our trauma and our failings, our rapes and our losses, bloodshed and undoing. People not from here often ask about the root of the Troubles. For a very long time, I struggled to join it all up, to make connections between the lines that history cast – as black as crows, as tall as ships – across my path.

Our kinfolk killed each other over a single oatcake during *an Gorta Mór* – the Great Hunger of the Irish Famine. My ancestors sent their children away to lands they knew they would never return from. My ancestors have watched themselves and those they held dear fade to bone before their eyes, shades of what they once had been. They watched their words lose all meaning – snuffed with the last of the light of all that they had once held true. How could we – the most recent offspring of folk who were put through this – have ever been expected to move on from it all without guidance? This level of inter-generational trauma takes time, so much time, to leave the gene pool. It surges through bloodlines like an ancient river.

This is our legacy of loss. We are – those of us born of this island – without any doubt, 'The Children of the Famine'. That Famine is, in my eyes, directly and intrinsically linked to the Troubles. That Famine reverberates even still, and I feel, inside my body, the ripples such loss leaves in its wake. Derry has one of the highest suicide rates in the UK, one of the lowest levels of breast-feeding, one of the highest obesity levels. The River Foyle has observed more loss in its time than I can even begin to comprehend. More of our lives in the North of Ireland have now been lost through suicide than were lost to the violence of the Troubles. How to even start to reshape a land that has spent centuries telling a dark story of loss? How to tell a new story of resilience and hope? Is this history of loss held in the soil? On the river itself? How can we honour the suffering of our ancestors – of those who came before us – but still try to unravel the chains we find ourselves bound by? Is the answer held within the very soil that failed them? Is the answer held in the residue the ghosts leave behind? The feathery ash of their snowy skin fluttering leeward, the blood that once swelled in their plumed veins seeping elsewhere, always coursing somewhere else. These days I am learning new ways through grief, different ways to hold it in my hands. I am trying, always trying, to honour those I have lost – no matter what the circumstances may have entailed.

The scale, and indeed *scéal*, the story, of Irish emigration in the port town of Derry remains, even to this day, without any proper or respectful record.

We *know*, in that old Irish way, of course, without it having ever been written down. It has been passed down, over and over, a palimpsest of loss: *eisimirce* – emigration.

We know as well as the fractured land.

We know as well as the land of other places. Places that had to expand, to make room inside hidden folds, to embrace our lost children when they turned up at their borders. We know as well as those children, those ones who have never known anything other than displacement.

We know in our bones, in our marrow and in our flesh.

We know in our skin and in our teeth.

We know in our bellies, deeper than that; we know in our guts.

We know in our wombs. We know in our births and in our unborn.

We know in our living and in our breathing.

We know in our leaving and in our dying.

We know in our sleep, in our dreams and in our spaces in between these.

We know in our thin places.

This year, the people of the port of Derry wait with bated breath to hear what their future holds, as a border town caught up in the trauma of Brexit without their votes ever having been regarded whatsoever. There is, as of yet, no solution for the 'problem' of our border: that invisible line we have never even seen. Recently family members of peaceful protestors whose lives were taken on Bloody Sunday – back when the Troubles began, on a day painted the blood-red of violence – were told only one person would be tried for the actions of many more. The past is a harrowing place; it drags us back, even as we try, ever deeper, to bury it. During an Extinction Rebellion March this year, in the same week as the Bloody Sunday trial, I took my place in Derry's Guildhall Square with dozens of other peaceful protestors, using our voices to speak for the future, for our planet, for our home. From where we stood we could see the River Foyle and the quay from which – not much more than a century and a half ago – we lost a million and a half of our kinfolk. The young lad leading the environmental rally on the steps of the Guildhall was the only representative from his school at the protest. He stood tall and defiant, upright against the biting winds, like that solo little egret in the silt, in the same place that the President of America had stood when I was a child.

This city is a city of history, he told us. If the river we are standing right beside floods in forty years' time when the temperatures have risen too high, we will lose that history. We stand together, the teenager told us, to preserve our history.

We all cheered, many of us screamed out at the top of our

lungs, some of us wept. We were thinking of those children, the children of our future – of our present: the ones who are making history. But as we cried out, some of us were also paying our respects to those children who were lost, the children of our past. We were mourning them, as we stood there; we were laying to rest all of those children born on the outer edges of history: those children lost to this land.

This year has been so full of political, social and environmental change. It feels like there is no steady ground beneath our feet. There are now only a few days left before the UK makes one of the biggest decisions of the century – which political party will be chosen to try to lead us all through this terrifying storm. A solo blackbird is singing its heart out in the tree opposite my house. It is a long-drawn-out song, the feel of which is nearing dirge-like, sorrowful, seeped in loss. We are losing things, that blackbird and me. We are all losing things. We are losing them every single day. One day, perhaps, I will go outside again, to this same sun-filled spot of concrete, on this quiet street in the heart of Derry, just a moment's walk from the River Foyle, to find this blackbird gone, vanished into deepest memory. I hope, deep to the core of my being, that that does not happen in my lifetime, or during the lifespan of any of us alive today, though we in this part of the world know better than to count any of our blackbirds before they are hatched. There is still hope though – so much hope, burrowed down deep inside so very many of us. No matter the political confusion, the ecological grief, the fear of the darkness ahead, we must leave room for that most human of all things: we must carve out room for hope. The last year in Derry I have experienced calm the like of which I never imagined I could know. It came gradually, that acceptance of this place, my hometown – that sense of moving along a path forwards, rather than being stuck in the mud of the past. If someone had told me that one day I would live happily in Derry, in a stable, loving relationship, I would never have believed them.

A few days ago I was outside my home, warming up to go for a run in St Columb's Park, and I was once more caught utterly off guard. The British Legion building is at the end of my street, and throughout my time here I have watched marching bands gather outside, flags of the red hand of Ulster and beer cans in tow, singing songs of the Queen and moments of Remembrance for past wars that saw such loss. I never, ever imagined that I could live so close to such extreme behaviour again, such a reminder of all that had played such a part in the division of this city, the aching sorrow that had been an outcome of the violence caused by fighting between Protestants and Catholics. A member of the Royal British Legion – an organisation that honours servicemen – struck up a conversation with me outside my front door. He was old, the man, and he was in pain. He talked to me of his hip replacement, of the loss of his freedom, of the unimaginable loneliness the death of his wife had brought him. He asked me what I did, and of my background, and he listened as I shared a little of the life I had lived a few streets away from where we stood. I could only see his eyes but I knew that there was no anger or resentment at all in either of our eyes. He told me how important meeting me was for him, and that he knew for sure that I will have a safe, peaceful life, that he knew that I will be okay. It shook me to my core when the old man told me that there is something in my eyes that is 'catching'. He said that it is actually more than in the eyes; 'it's in what's behind the eyes'. He walked slowly towards his car. He looked back, beaming – and said goodbye, and I knew it then.

It is time to leave. The old man has given me permission, in a way, to look to the future. I know it, and I know – deep inside of me – that I can never un-know it. I know that the time has come for me to leave this city. I am being called to another place, to other places, and now – for the first time, properly – the time is right for me to leave. I am ready. The peace I so desperately needed to make – here, with this place where I was born – is made. I don't know when exactly, or how, it happened – I know only the where of it: the acceptance and forgiveness happened inside *me*, as much as in this oak-fringed place. Yes, this broken, beautiful city has changed in the decades since I was born but the crucial changes – the ones that let me know that I am ready to leave – happened in spaces that cannot quite be mapped. It has been a long time in the sculpting, this sense of letting go, of making space inside for healing – and I will do everything in my power to shelter the hollow inside me I have carved. I will not run from here in anger, fear or helplessness. I am only leaving because the time has come. I have no more space for violence or for destruction, for fear and uncertainty; I have grieved already for my city, as

much as I can. I am leaving so the space inside me is kept safe.
So that *I* am kept safe, too.

I reach the park just as the afternoon light has reached the
dip in the hill. I watch as it casts its shafts onto the old hawthorn
tree standing alone in its muddy field. I listen as the wrens flit
from branch to branch, as the hooded crows call to the soft
blue quietude of the sky. I let the small, curved part of the
back of me lean into the V of the middle of the tree, in a way
I haven't done since I was a wee girl. It feels, all at once, like
an exact fit – as though I am supposed to be here, as though
maybe I don't need to move from this exact spot, ever. I want
to see how we look – if there are any big gaps I am unaware
of, or if I am nestled into the V of this tree as tightly as I think
I am. I want someone else to look, and to tell me if how I
feel is real, is valid – but there is no one else around. I am
alone but for the crows and the wrens, the blackbirds and
mistle-thrushes, the wrens and blue tits, two squirrels and a
single magpie. The light has changed, hurriedly; it is on its way
home, so I make for mine, too – the rented house I am making
ready, now, to leave. I slide my body out of the dip in the
hawthorn, wet bark under hand, autumn leaves underfoot, and
walk back up the hill. The light throws itself down onto the
wee hill beside the statue of Columcille and the dove, and I
look to the circle of oak trees to the right. I follow the light
around to the walled garden – strewn with rubbish, grass burnt,
stone walls graffitied with republican threats – and there in the
muck, beside a dead hedgehog, is a small mammal skull. A
beautiful, sculpted thing of grace: a reminder of the way that

our bodies – the bodies of us all – are full of bone, solid and as white as a dancing moth. You are blood and bone, as I am; we are the stuff of blood and bone, the stuff of life and death, and all that we are met by in between.

I leave the skull, one of the most exquisite things I have ever found, and think of what is held within this place, this ancient wood of oaks in an equally ancient city. It is a place that has been so important for me, and I wonder what trace – if any – I may have left here upon this land. I wonder if it can be felt in any way by another – human, badger, bird, moth – by those both made of bone, and not. Any of us can experience a thin place. Some of us will be called towards them – over and over again – as though a bell is being rung for us. Others might never experience a thin place in their lifetime. I only know how my own experiences have been. I can only share the way that my own insides feel when I am standing in a place that drags me away from sorrow and fear. Places create ripples inside of us; they rise and they swell inside each of us in turn; how we experience place is completely unique to us alone. I have had wildly varied experiences at Shroove from one day to the next. I have come away, on occasion, feeling almost bereft that *it* didn't come – that sense of being both out of, and entirely in, myself and my surroundings. I searched – anxiety and doubt growing in me like ashes from a fire long gone out – to no avail. There are days when it will not be what you want it to be. The veil will be thicker than mud on some days. All things flow and change; this much we all know. They course through this world, gently trickling on some mornings, bursting through the banks in terrifying, powerful waves on others. Nothing – not a single person, thing or place – remains the same for ever.

Thin places are safe spaces, where we are given the chance to be alone, to pause – a gift we find ourselves being given less and less. There is room, more room than we might normally have, to wonder. Room to ponder what lies beyond the life we are used to leading, the everyday pumping of blood through veins. Places to wonder what it means to be made up of blood and sinew, and what – aside from carved, delicate white bone – might be left of us after we are gone, if anything.

I am thinking now, really thinking, about blood. How it charts a path inside us that we cannot ever really see, how it ties things all up with thin red thread, how we do not choose it – how we never really lose it, though we may try in vain. It is in the *veins,* too, like a dream of time, a cinnabar moth, in the places where the sinew tries to hide.

December, full of holly, hips and robins, marches on. As the days make the shadows stand taller, and taller still, the land is red with robins, and I am grateful for them, so grateful; the winter still holds red breasts – and those red breasts still hold a song. I think now, almost every single day, about the hedgerows of this land. Of all that they have lost, of all that they still hold close.

The cold outside my window has taken a different shape as the land curves towards the winter solstice. I find myself thinking about a day long gone by, across that border, the one that none of us has actually seen. It has been a very long time since I thought about that day, the day my brother and I were followed, in the midst of dark, terrifying, violent times, to the cove at Kinnagoe Bay by a blood-red, flame-tailed gift of a fox. Of how we took him as a thing given to us in place of the one we had just lost: our father. I wonder when the last time was that I really sat and thought about my brother's little-boy face, the way his voice used to sound, the way he looked when he fell asleep on the drive home like he always did.

Something deep down has shifted, and with that quiet change, a space has been carved inside me; there is room now for things, for things that there once was no place for before.

•

My island is one more colour, too, one that we cannot ever forget. A colour that shows itself best of all when it is set against a backdrop of white – against snow and ice – against bog-cotton in places not quite barren. Against all things that have not yet been hurt or broken, against the wood white butterfly as she dreams her way through the Burren.

This island, my island, is red. It is the colour of fire and of blood, of anger and war, of brutal strength and of warning.

It is the colour that shouts of courage in the dark.

## CHAPTER TWELVE

### *Hollowing, Hallowing*

THERE ARE PLACES THAT DANCE around us – like moths drawn to the light of a flame from a fire just making ready to take its leave, or that may, in fact, have never even been lit at all.

There are places that will not be pinned to any wall, no matter how exquisite their colourful, near-celestial markings.

There are places where space and time do not, can not, *will not* exist within the confines we have so keenly tried to erect here for ourselves – on this our solid ground, here on our carved-out lands.

There are places that are so beyond what we claim to know is true as to make them almost imagined, mythical in that way of labyrinths and nymphs, of unimaginable beasts, of stepping in the same body of water twice. Of curses and twisted things, of lost humans and found objects, of forgetting and forging, casting out and dragging down, of the power of naming and speaking it out loud on the highest hill to be found. Of holes and caves and caverns and nooks. Of crossing points and meeting mounds and halfway hillocks, of the in-between that maybe holds the still point. Places that sing of all that came, of all that is here and all that will come.

Places that speak in tongues, in stillness, in those delicate, moth-light ways that cannot quite ever be silenced.

•

What does it mean to come from a hollowed-out place? What becomes of a person, when the mark left by the highest spring tide is still not a safe enough place to build?

To hollow out is to remove the inside of something: to make an empty space in the place of something else. Sometimes, there is space inside us but no matter how we may want it, nothing grows there.

*Hollow* has an Old English root, *holh* – hole or hollow place.

There is frost on the ground in the heart of winter but in my mind I am back on a fire-bright day half a year back. It is the end part of June 2019. I am *across the border*. I have followed the gently carved meanderings of the River Foyle from my hometown – past Culmore Point at first, then Quigley's Point – to the body of water's western banks at Moville, where the Bredagh River flows into the sea. Moville has two possible Gaelic origins: *Bun an Phobail* – 'Foot of the Parish' and *Magh Bhile* – 'Plain of the Ancient Tree'. Cooley Stones and Skull House are the most ancient sites – taken by Christian monastic settlers and repurposed as a cross and a graveyard – when such things were introduced to this northerly corner of the island,

likely by St Finian in this instance. I am camping on the ethereal banks of the Bredagh River, at Glencrow, beneath the
tallest trees I have ever known. I have never seen so many
crows in my life. They craekk and craw, and they gather themselves into a murder above the oldest bridge in Ireland, built
by the hands of St Patrick many midsummers ago.

I am at a staggeringly northern point, but I am in *the South*.

On my first day here alone, I take myself along the river,
past blackbirds that sing of the long-gone past, through a
meadow that catches the sun as it ebbs out of the June-pink
sky. I am on my third day away from the internet. I take no
images on my phone of the elderflower and the butterflies, the
dipper and the mating insects I cannot name, the folkloric
copse and the cinematic coastline as it comes into view. I am
off Instagram, Facebook and Twitter for a while. I will not be
releasing these whispers of moments out into the ether as any
post or insta-story; no tweets will pin this moment to any wall.
I want to see how it feels to just *be* in this place.

I have been battling with my own self for most of the year
when it comes to motherhood. I've been thinking how some
of us are not properly mothered. How some of us are unable
to be mothers. How sometimes the two things come together,
and there is nothing we can do except make peace with it and
with ourselves. I've been slowly trying to unravel the idea of
child and mother – nature and nurture – and allowing the
grief to take its natural course. There are ways to mother beyond
what we often hold as the real or proper way. Equally, we can
be mothered by those who are not our blood, by those we

have never met. We can mother our own self, if we will only allow ourselves.

I walk alone along the shoreline and I think of all those who have stood on these sandy banks before me, in the shadows of coffin ships and unimaginable, inherited grief.

From 1873 onwards emigrants leaving their starved, broken corner of the world through the port of Derry were carried down the Foyle to the spot on which I stand to join the Allan and Anchor steamship lines. The liners could be seen by those they had left behind as they passed along this coastline en route to America or Canada. If there was a local person emigrating, it was customary to light a bonfire on O'Donnell's Hill, just above where I am rooted, so that it was visible to the passing ship: a farewell of light.

What does it mean to hallow a place?

When we hallow a place, we bless it and we make it holy. We sanctify and honour it; we consecrate and hold it as sacred. We keep its ways and we hold them close. We listen to the place and we feel its reverberations in our bones.

St John's Day is celebrated nearing the close of June – marking the birth of John the Baptist. The night before is linked to the summer solstice and is known as '*bone fire night*' in many parts of Ireland. *Tine Fhéile Eoin* – St John's Eve fires – were originally lit as part of a Celtic celebration to honour the goddess Áine, who was associated with the sun, fertility and the protection of crops and animals. However, as with many pagan festivals, the Catholic Church took over the event and linked it to the birth of St John.

On St John's Eve, the veil between the worlds is lifted entirely. White cats appear as women, folk dance themselves into different forms, and it is said that the fairies play sweet music and entice the people to come with them to their caves. The people who leave on this night never ever come back again.

This St John's Eve, on my first night camping in this haunting place since I went sober, I sleep in a crow-straight line in the direct view of an ancient fairy ring. My ancestors would have prayed by the fire for the land and good weather on this date. If they did not offer such prayer, a bad harvest would surely come, and the white trout would not come back up the river as they were wont to with the midsummer floods. And so I kneel alone in prayer: a prayer to the mother of the land, a prayer to all those who came before. A friend arrives and we tend the fire until the night has given way to the day. We talk of history, of borders, of womenhood, of ritual and of place; we talk of hope.

We awake the following morning, on St John's Day, and we swim in the belly of the Atlantic at Shroove Beach beneath the lighthouse, underneath a sky full of oily-skinned cormorants in low flight. That day would have once been the day on which swimming began that year for my ancestors, and as we swim I feel safe in the knowledge that the keeping of this ritual might offer us two protection from drowning for the full year ahead. Silence passes between my friend and me. I watch as she is held within the arms of the thinnest place I know. I dip in and out – of place, the water, of the wind as it calls each of our names beneath the summer rain.

We walk the shore path from Greencastle towards Moville, gathering driftwood for the fire in the cove at the foot of the home of a writer we both admire, Brian Friel. We feel his presence with us as we gather, his hand steadying us as we think of what lies ahead of us both in the coming months of the impending Brexit. My friend in London, and I here – in this hollowed-out, hallowed place, a place that has known such haunting, reverberating loss.

My friend leaves, and once more I am alone by the fire. Leaving the ashes from last night where they are, I build on top: crisscrossing the sticks, leaving space for the bones I will place into the hollow later.

My ancestors were well aware of the effects of fire. Mastering this element had changed their lives, although they knew it was a thing fraught with danger. Homes then were temporary dwellings, and could be burned to the ground in the time it took to return from the well. The sun was considered to bring great healing energy. Walking three times 'sun-wise', or *cor deiseil*, around a fire represented the circling of the sun, and was a potent ritual invocation of the sun's healing power. I walk around the fire – one that I myself lit – three times, on St John's Day this year, and I think of the circles we all walk, over and over. I think of what it means to really let go of something. Of what it means to fall back into the curve of a place, and to let it hold you. The Irish word for fire, *tine*, is closely linked with *tinfeadh*, the Irish word for inspiration, and for breathing. I think of what these two things need, of what kindles them. I think of what it might mean to leave a place through choice, rather than through force, or through fire.

Bone fires have been lit in this place for centuries, and the ashes and embers have been used to purify the space for just as long. Bones of our ancestors, keeping us safe in the hollow of their hands. This year it was confirmed that bones washed up on a beach in Canada are those of Irish famine victims. They are the human remains of twenty-one individuals, unearthed over a five-year period, from the 1847 *Carricks* shipwreck. The ship left Sligo carrying 180 passengers fleeing the Famine, but it sank, drowning at least 150 of those on board. Fragile skeletal remains of three boys – two aged seven and one eleven-year-old – suggest rural Irish origins based on severe malnutrition shown in the salt-wearied bones.

My St John's fire this year could be seen from most points of Glencrow, a signal of a form. I have been thinking so much, since then, of beacons. Classically, beacons were fires lit at well-known locations on hills or high places, used either as lighthouses to lead folk to safety or for signalling over land that enemies were approaching. Systems of this kind have existed for centuries over much of the world. Beacons have also allegedly been abused by ship-wreckers. A fire placed where it should not be placed would be used to direct a ship against shoals or beaches so that its cargo could be looted after the ship sank or ran aground. The fall of Troy was signalled by a chain of eight beacons burning on the shore to send the news across to Clytemnestra in Argos.

From where my friend and I stand that June day on the

shore, Ballykelly – that village where I spent my teens, the place where I lost my friend to an act of devastating violence – can be seen across the water. The fires we lit many moons ago to fuel our nights of teenage angst would have been a beacon visible on the other side of the shore in Donegal.

Beacons, fires, lighthouses: what message, what signal are our ancestors sending us across the waters between us and them, then and now? What signal are we sending to those in front of us on the other shore?

The first time I became aware of fire being used for something other than comfort, I was battling my way through its inky, thick smoke – an eleven-year-old girl – whose home had just been bombed. For decades that coal-black crow I met there followed me around like the smell of smoke on young, not yet woken-up, skin.

I think about it all; I take every single shard of it and I hold it all in my shaky, sooty hands. I think of how I taught myself, just this year – alone, in a different, equally cold Derry house – how to light my first fire.

How even after enduring a history in which fire brought terror and destruction – a flame-red thread that burned through my crimson bloodline – I found the way back to the flames across a different threshold.

I think about how – even though my story is laced with fear, the kind that maybe only fire can instill – I found a way to jump the embers of the past, to teach my willing hands the way to tend to a hearth.

I think about the fact that the first fire I ever lit outside was on St John's Eve – a night when the veil between worlds is lifted – in a delicate and echoing thin place. The first fire I lit outdoors, in that raw, boundless world, was tended by my own self alone.

There are places in this luminous, aching world that are glassy, like the lakes of a hundred years. They are both the mirror and they are the light that you seek with which to find them. There are places that I know – in the exterior and hardened parts of my bones – are in fact *the fire itself.* There are places that are both hollowed and hallowed all in one. These places are like snowfall in darkness – sensed without being seen – we swim through their veil like fireflies on the solstice.

They are not ours but we are theirs. We are *of*, not in, them. We are – for the most celestial and ancient moment – a part of those places ourselves.

I think about my grandfather, and the abandonment I feel he experienced. I think of mine, too, of all those things I am only now beginning to give voice to. I think of my grandfather's mother, and of my own. Of how sometimes walking away from someone, cutting the roots, finally makes the space for healing. I think of how even a mother can abandon her child, and how even a child can learn a way through that. I think of all the words that, in this echoing moment, are still flightless birds. All those things that still sit, patiently, quietly, at my feet. I think of them stretching out their wings, testing the air closest to us. I think of them waiting for the wind to settle down upon the land. I think of the sky – patient, too – waiting for these unspoken things to be sent up, out of silence, into the space where they will fly.

These thin and sacred places wait for us to *remember*.

I think about the bones of my ancestors, on whichever shore they may or may not wash up.

I think about my own bones – pieces of me – that still hold the imprint of generations before me, folk that saw such sorrow.

I think about my family, about the way it has been broken up like a china cup. I think about the fragments of us – embedded in mud-coated fields, on forgotten windowsills of places we do not wish to return to, and in the silted bed of the sea. I think about the way that some of these parts have been glued back together, then smashed apart again, repeated fractures creating lines both visible and invisible – making a border of the red of my bloodline. I think about how some of these shattered parts might be lost to me for ever, buried beneath the weight of all that we have gone through, under all of the pain that has never been acknowledged – beside all of those things that must be carried out of silence, if they hope to ever be put right.

I think about how, if one of those bones of mine was found on a shoreline, I would want it to be burned on St John's. I think about the fact that I have let go of so much, that I may never again see my own mother. I think about the fact that I likely will never be a mother, either. I see my body then for what it is – blood and bone. White pieces of porcelain on a shoreline, light as feather, sculpted as stone. I would want my bones to become ash in the belly of a fire, to be placed back into the earth from which I had been formed. To be scattered over field and threshold, to bring protection, healing and nourishment, to be a beacon for all those still left on the shore, a flicker of dancing light for all of those who stayed.

## CHAPTER THIRTEEN

## *Éin Bhána* – White Birds

Here is now.

Here is then.

Here is everything, and everywhere, that stands between.

DECEMBER HAS ARRIVED, FILLING THE land with red berries that dot the hedgerows; the night skies are dark, full of frost and stars. The winter solstice that is on the way – close enough to nearly make out through the morning mist – will bring the year to a close, a year of deep and unimaginable change for this island, for me and for the path that lies ahead for us all. Through the window, as dawn breaks like a newly born creature, I watch wee drops of rain, collected on the pane during the night, begin to make their way back down to the soil beneath. There is no real light in the garden so far to speak of; the sun is nowhere to be found down here, yet. When I woke up this morning, long before the sun came up, the first frost had settled in onto the grey of the ground. The winter sky was still as black as a freshly fallen night; no real sounds could be heard above the morning's stillness.

I have woken up in a place that I have only slept in a handful of times: an old stone railway cottage in the very heart of Ireland, many miles from Derry. It is so much more than a border that I have crossed to move here, to simply *be* here, in this wild, silent and ancient place. This place is a world away from Derry, from the part of the North where I was born, and it is somewhere I intend to stay; it is the first place that has ever felt like home. I have spent so little time here, since I left that city that I first ran from – then ran to. So little time has passed since I left the city that both birthed my suffering and held the space for me to start to heal.

The Derry I have only just left is not the same Derry I moved back to three and a half years ago, which was almost unrecognisable from the Derry I fled from many years before. I try to think about the future for that shape-shifting city on the banks of the River Foyle. I try to imagine the curves and bends, the growth and the change, the meandering journey that I know must lie ahead. It will not be an easy journey for the city; it never has, nor could be. But I trust that all will be well, I feel it in a part of me I cannot quite locate. Those oaks along the banks of that beautiful city have witnessed so much; they have stood tall, firmly rooted; the people their canopies guard are a kind unlike any I have met elsewhere, in any other place I have wandered. I don't know what it is that makes Derry people how they are, in all their layers and strata – a palimpsest of ache and deep resilience. Is it something in our soil, born in the ancient roots beneath our feet? Is it something carried in the flow of that fiercely hungry, incomparably beautiful river? Is it something that seeped into those sacred stones, rock that held fast against raging, burning winds, and against the blood, against the tears? The places we are from do not define us, they do not make us, they do not root us, they cannot hold this earth from its inescapable turning. The places that we run to, where we try to find the means to simply stay alive, to stay *here* on this hard, gorgeous earth, those places that hold us tight and that let us see a way out – a way back *in* – are much the same as the places that we came from. They are much the same as any place, in any corner of this tender, glorious, astonishing world.

Places do not heal us; they do not take the suffering we have known and bury it in their bellies. Places do not gather the broken parts of us up and stitch them back together. Places do not make the light shine on crow-black nights. Places do not take away our sorrow; they do not unearth the words buried under frozen bog-land; they do not call the birds back when they have been long gone from our sky.

Places do not heal us.

Places only hold us; they only let us in.

Places only hold us close enough that we can finally see ourselves reflected back.

Last night the sky here at midnight was almost unreal. The frost moon shone down from the folklore-blue body of sky above this place, constant and as white as snow. I have never before seen a sky as full of everything both known and unknown. I have never before known a path as brightly lit by only the night sky, by the full white moon alone. No darkness fell on the fields, or on me as I walked them – mud underfoot, nothing at all held within my cupped hands. Earlier yesterday, under a sun that was bleeding out into the soft, still fields – purple and grey haze painting themselves onto a cold amber sky – I watched starlings for longer than I ever have before. Their bodies – like the tall, quiet trees – made silhouettes in the early evening sky, dancing together in perfect harmony, grace dripping off wings that – if I had been closer – would have glistened and shone, gifts of muscle and feather.

There are no starlings on this frost-grey morning, and I wonder where they are now, where they spent the lunar-bright night. I spent it in this new home, a tiny stone railway cottage built – like the border I have crossed to get to it – almost a century ago, in the year 1921. The cottage, this laneway – all of this beating, wild life that I am so completely surrounded by now – feels like a gift, too. They feel like something I will be grateful for, always; something that *anyone* in this sad, confusing, lonely world, in this world that gives us so much beauty it makes us ache, would be grateful for. There are few words that I can form in these early days in this new place that can even try to do any of it justice. It is wet – so wet that muck takes on shades and textures I have never before known. This laneway – no more 'mine' than the folk of the other four houses I now share it with – is so out of the way (*'of where?'* I hear so many folk I admire whisper in my young ear; *'outta the way o' where exactly?*') that there is no WiFi signal, no post-code and hardly a phone signal of which to speak. It is, quite literally, in the heart of Ireland. It is, this place I have found myself in, like most of the midlands, so flat that you can see for miles on top of country miles. I still catch myself looking out for curves, and for rough, craggy lines. It is, of course, the farthest-most place in this whole wave-sculpted island from the sea. When M inherited the cottage, two summers back, I knew precisely what I was talking of when I whispered of it being 'out of the way'. That raw, ancient Atlantic Ocean – the liquid backdrop to some of the thinnest places I have ever encountered – will never be further from my reach at any place on this island than when I am *here*, in this cottage. I will never be further from my favourite body of water – the one that held me over the last three years, like I was a thing worth saving – than when I am on this small, quiet stretch of land.

When M first found out the cottage was being left to him, his initial reaction was that we would likely try to clear it, fix it up, and sell it. That first summer, we drove there as many weekends as we could, leaving Derry after work and arriving as the sun set over brambles and abandoned workhouses, barns full of old machinery and swallows, surrounded by insects that caught the light and stayed with us as we slept in our van beside the house. We'd waken to the fields full of gold and silence, the hedgerows steeped in birdsong and colour, our own selves full of deep, undeniable gratitude. The more time we spent there, exploring the area, walking the laneway and the fields around it, assessing the damage that had been done to the house over the decade it had lain empty, the more difficult we found it to take ourselves back up the road – across the border – to our rented house in the urban heart of Derry. Life in the city was the best we could make of it with little money after paying our bills each month, only two friends living close enough to spend any time with, and never having enough time to do the things we so much wanted to do. We were working long hours in our café, constantly struggling to make ends meet, and finding that all we wanted to do on our day off was go back to the cottage. It wasn't about running away from the problems in the North, my desire to be at the cottage, nor was it about attempting to forget the ghosts of my past in the town where I was born. It wasn't worry, or fear, or hurt, that ache I experienced when I was away from Correaly. Even before this house had a ceiling, a kitchen or any form of heating, it felt like the safest place I'd ever known. Neither of us really remembers the moment we decided we would leave Derry and move to this place, or which of us it was who first shared how tied we felt to it. This place that, somehow, in some way, makes me feel like putting down roots.

The past is a place not dissimilar to many others on this island, the veil between that distant place and this present one can be as thin as ice on a lake. The veil may be thin, but it is still there, nonetheless. The past is exactly that, and we can never bring it back up from under any surface it dwells beneath. We live in these days that we have – these days that we still have left – and we live these days with those things we still have left, too. No matter what we try to do, any actions that we take, any way in which we choose to speak of things – the past remains in another place: that other world, in which its roots are firmly planted. After winter the spring will come, and a whole different world will be there outside this window, a view I have yet to see. I know the horses will be gone, and with them the seven Connemara ponies that have woken me through these long, howling nights of December. They will leave, and in their place there will be other things – other creatures – maybe there will be some that I have never seen before.

In the summer, a handful of months ago, this whole laneway was full of things in flight: butterflies, moths, dragonflies and damselflies. And I still cannot quite believe I am really remembering it all right, when I think about the swallows, of how they lifted up from all the parts of the house, from all the parts of the lane, how it felt like they had come from all the edges of the land, just to be there on that bright, still afternoon. I will never forget how many swallows dipped and dived above us that day, as we started to clear away all the broken things and overgrown thorn bushes to make a path through the garden. That was almost half a year ago, a handful of days after I camped in Donegal at St John's as the full summer sun bled out from a northerly sky. Just last month, in this icy cold winter, I returned to Shroove to have my last swim there, for how long I am not quite sure. It was the last swim I would have there while living in my hometown, the last of this year of such vast change – the last before I moved across the border.

It was a swim to mark a full year sober in this the year that held the most change I have ever known, a year that threw more onto my path than any of the other years of this life so far. There was no one else there when I arrived, and I spent the whole time completely alone. The winds were soft, like bog-cotton, and the whole sky above me was tinged with coppery pink. I made ready for the water, and waited for the tallest wave to drag me under; I was making the most of the Atlantic's raw, healing energy. I was just about to become much less able to make my way there, into its tender, salty grip.

I thought of all that had gone before, of a life lived, the paths taken, as best I could. I cried and I didn't wipe the tears away; I wondered where the sea would carry them to, when I left. I thought of the future – of mine, of yours, of all of ours. Of all that it holds. Of all that will be gained, and lost. I lay back onto the winter water's surface, and I floated, waiting for the cormorants to pass over me one by one – waning, like the moon – like how we are watching the ice melt away, helpless and terrified. I thought about the way that loss in our world is multiplying, magnifying, about how we need to learn how to hold it all close, closer than we ever have before, close enough that we can see, again. I knew then what it was that had changed, what it is that these places have somehow done to me.

It was icy cold in the sea's belly, and so I left when I knew the time had come, and returned back out to the grip of the land, the hold of solid ground. As I made to leave the beach, I cast my eyes down onto the shelf that the storm waves had made in the sand. There, right in the dip – where the curve made a mountain-top out of a few centimetres of wet sand – a hag stone lay in waiting. I knew that that gift of sea and stone – of here and there, then and now, and all that lies between – was meant, was sent for me.

Hag stones, with their perfect hole, are held to be highly sacred objects. They have been called by many names over the centuries: witch stones, adder stones, snake eggs, hex stones, fairy stones, holy stones, holeys and eye stones. The stone has been created by the water – birthed and moulded by it – and as such is an extension of it, retaining the healing power of the sea within its form. In effect, a hag stone is an amulet of protection, and so much more. People often find hag stones at turning points in their lives, as the circle turns, as people, periods or places ebb away from them, leaving the gap that holds the promise of something new.

We are called back to places that, in times of difficulty, hold the power to give us what we need to get through. This story began at a wild cove in Donegal, forty miles across a hard border from Derry, two and a half decades ago. A wild red fox followed a little girl whose father had just moved out of her house from the top of a hill full of wild hedgerows and butter-flies to an uninsured, beat-up car on the Atlantic shoreline.

That day, for the first time, the little girl filled her hands with unidentifiable bones, sticks stripped bare of their bark and a single sea-rounded stone: found things from an echoing place to bring home with her, in the place of all that had been lost.

The summer is past, and the autumn that followed has been,

and has gone, too. Winter has most definitely reached this laneway, as it had reached Shroove that day as I swam, and it is leaving the traces of itself all around. Mornings have arrived here, in this isolated corner of the land, that have been full of pink and red light, orange and gold swimming through the clouds like soft lines, winter's delicate sky veins. Not today, though; this morning is all grey and heavy, all full of the need to draw in close to the hearth, a raw reminder of the strength of this, the year's last season. The railway track just in front of the cottage – the reason the cottage was built at all – is looking more like the ghost line that it is, on this dark December morning, than it ever could in the glow of summer.

Yesterday, beneath a morning moon, low and white, hanging in a winter-blue sky, I stood under an old, gnarly thorn tree as a solo robin hopped about my feet in a sodden field. I followed the line he made on the muddy surface with my eyes, from here to there, and back again, then up, then off, now – away. When he had gone, I followed his line with my feet as well as my eyes, with my legs dragging my body through thick bog-muck, full of the past, full of things we may never quite understand. At the point in the field where he had left me to tread this new stretch of land alone, there was something black and solid, something other than winter grass and peat-brown bog-water. I placed my hands over it, tracing the curved lines that ran across its form like waves – an ebb and flow the kind of which I had never before set eyes on. Bog-oak, sculpted over thousands of years by the weight of what it has known, in the place where it has lain.

I left it there, and quickly made my way back to the gate at the top of the field, just as sleet began to turn the field pewter grey, thrown across by a wind that had been hidden in the trees. As quickly as the sleet had come, the sky was full to bursting above my head with armfuls of mistle-thrushes, calling and dragging storm-light in their wings. They landed, chaotic, cinematic, all at once, despite the howling winds. I ran back into the wind that bit and barged, to the earth beneath the thorn tree, and lifted the ancient black wood from the part of the field where it had been spat out. I lifted it and I brought it back with me – across the field, up the laneway, into my home. I am still that wee girl, with her eyes open to this turning, aching earth. I still feel it all, every single part of it, deeper than my bones. Wing-beats above a concrete council estate, snow-light on blossom after violence, moth-light on a red fox after loss – I am still that wee girl seeking beauty in the murk.

Three years after moving back to my hometown of Derry on the Irish border that grew and grew in fame and importance, I was given the chance to leave the place behind in an entirely different way from how leaving had always looked before. In the past I had felt as if there were no options at all, that the only way through it all – through the sorrow, confused identity and the worried anger – was to leave. Coming from a city so permeated by division, a place so defined by violence and loss, having your roots in a place that made you feel scared and lonely most of the time made leaving feel like the path of least resistance. Every single time I left any other place –

Dublin, Cork, Edinburgh, Bristol – it always felt just the same as leaving Derry, as though the decision was never really one to be made; the leaving had been writ in stone long before. Sadness, trauma and unquantifiable loss had shaped me into a person who never really allowed themselves to become rooted anywhere at all. I carried the memory of my roots being severed (so often, too many times by far) around with me like a heavy weight I thought I deserved to have been burdened with. I never really saw the things I experienced as things that I might have needed some help with, as things that maybe I could actually unload, and never pick back up again. As things that maybe had never really been mine to carry in the first place.

I spent most of my life feeling – harrowing as it is to admit, now – that I somehow must have deserved these things: they were mine, and to shed them would be to shed *me*, in turn. As though the thing that best defined me was the suffering and the sorrow, the things I had seen, and the things I had lost. I could not, for decades, even try to imagine that there might be something in underneath it all, that there might be a self that would remain no matter how many layers I might slowly learn to undo. I had never before really accepted that I was a person who fled from place to place, thing to thing, person to person, without ever staying long enough to settle. When people accused me of running away, of being emotionally cold, of so many things that I now see were absolutely right, I placed the blame on anything and everything else around me. I never took responsibility for my own part in it all; I accepted the role of victim and I was happy to play it the best I could. I understand now that there are things that burrow inside of us and take years to unearth, to free ourselves from. That, in time, trust and hope might take the place of other things: things that we never, ever deserved to have to carry.

Light finds its own places, the spaces for it to take as its own; the black crow of sorrow can not, will not, keep the light under its sooty wing for ever. Change comes, and growth follows in its wake. You awake one morning, and the fog has lifted, entirely, as though it had been a thin and delicate veil. One moment you were held by the dark, thick mud of the past, unable to see any way through, and the next you were floating on a glassy, echoing lake. You see yourself now, reflected in the water, and you see strength along with softness; you see someone who is ready, now – so ready – to see.

Time, on the delicate, dusty wing of a white moth, must and will fly on. Memories dance and move like silken ghosts; sometimes we can see them and *only* them, and at others we are left alone to be fully and firmly in the present. To choose paths based on feelings other than sorrow and fear. To allow ourselves to find the way through.

The farmer's voice, when it comes, is soft and kind; he wears gentleness in his words, somehow. I am back in this cold December morning, looking at the old railway tracks that we had both heard the owl fly over just last night, looking at the track-marked field with the farmer, really *looking*. Cows fed, field observed, words shared – he leaves, and it is just me in the laneway once more. The tall trees – ivy and finch-covered

– line the bottom part of the laneway, towering down over the wee grey cottage like they are protecting it from something unseen, held up there in the sky. The grey of the house's stone, set in its firm place between those trees and the wild hedgerow, red rosehips popping out like sparks – makes a countryside Christmas card out of the scene. No one has spent a Christmas – a winter at all – in that cottage for over a decade. All around it, blackthorn and whitethorn, nettles and sprawling rosebushes, red berry and brambles compete with one another for light that isn't quite here, yet, on this grey December morning. To the left of the cottage – right outside the original front door – is the rotted, broken remains of what was once wooden decking. The first time I visited the cottage this year, when walking through the garden to follow the path of a peacock butterfly (the first I'd set eyes on for decades), the whole middle section of that decking gave way completely, the damp wood dragging me down towards the rich soil beneath. I was covered in bruises and cuts, stings and scratches; it felt like someone or something – the previous owner, the house itself, the place? – was asking me if I was really there, if I was really in the place properly. It was almost the opposite experience of being in a thin place. There was no sense whatsoever, on that first day in this new house, of floating out of myself, no otherworldly, dream-like feel; I was being reminded instead that I was absolutely and completely in that exact place, at that specific time. There was no leaving to be had when I fell through those very real – utterly material – gaps. The blood gushed and the allergic bumps began to prickle the surface of my skin almost immediately; I was there, in that moment, and I remember feeling more aware of being alive than I had felt for quite some time.

This morning, a perfect V of whooper swans flew above the lane – creamy white, and carrying ancient lore. The year my childhood home almost burned to the ground – with us all sound asleep inside – was the same year that I encountered whooper swans for the first time, the creatures I feel most drawn to in times of need. It was less than a month after the bombing. We were driving to get petrol – across the border – in the silken half-light of autumn. We were right at the mouth of the land-bridged island, just before Fahan, when the sound came . . . a sound I have never managed to get out of my head. Wing-beats like the beginning of life, or like the very ending of it, like all of the moments held in between. *Eala glórach* – whooper swan, its name meaning 'noisy swan' – but when I think back to that unnerving sight of the first whooper swan I ever saw taking to the air above us in all her ethereal beauty, it is the silence that she left in her wake that lingers the most. The sense that something does not have to be a thing of terror and sorrow, of trauma and loss, to move us into the depths of quietude. The knowledge, all at once, sent down from an unknown place like muddied, perfect feathers – that silence does not always have to speak of things that cannot be said. The sense that there are things that can move us to silence, to an inner place – neither here nor there – to warm and necessary tears, that are actually *beautiful* things. She went higher that October day, decades ago; I remember the guttural honking being so suddenly – so fully – replaced by silence. I stood, echoing the swan's chosen way; no more words left me that day for quite some time.

Whooper swans find great refuge in the places close to Derry. I read that in 1995, the year the petrol bomb came through my bedroom window, more of them wintered on Lough Swilly than anywhere else in the UK or Ireland. That swan I encountered was one of thousands that had made a long, hard journey, over land and sea, through weather both varied and treacherous to seek shelter on the shores that I was also enveloped in that year. That winter I shared company with so many of those creatures on the hill overlooking the River Foyle. All of us were still on a journey of a form, each seeking safe harbour – a place to call home – until the next wind called us up and away.

My overarching memory of that year was encountering my first whooper swan, making for the sky above Inch Island. I have never quite lost the sound of those powerful, folkloric wings beating; the echoing, learned silence she carried with her into the early autumn sky is still with me, even today.

•

There is still an imagined, ghost-laden line running through the land that formed me, cutting across the surface of the sorrow-laden, resilient island I love so well. Oystercatchers still sing their siren songs on both sides of that border. Now I have found myself living on a real ghost-line. Our new home lies on the only section of the old railway line where any part of the track is still visible. It is the line that once connected the South and the North, faded at every other part of the journey it once carried trains along. The house, and the line outside our front door, are reminders, traces, of so much that has been lost. I cannot help but offer a prayer when I look at the old sleepers and the rusting metal, desperately hoping that the Brexit negotiations follow a path that allows mutual respect, each for the other, on both sides of that troubled border.

Not far from here, just past where the swans have likely now already landed, is the Hill of Uisneach. When I finally decided to move here, away from Derry, away from the North, into the very heart of the island, I read about the land I was coming to – a place I knew almost nothing about. I learned that the area all around this quiet laneway is an incredibly sacred place. Since prehistoric times, the Hill of Uisneach has been the great assembly for the tribes and kings of Ireland. It was here that laws were made and disputes settled. The hill is a place of energy and renewal; people have been drawn here for over 5,000 years. It was the seat of the High Kings, a sacred site of worship, and the place where St Patrick built the burial ground for Ériu, the goddess after whom Ireland was named.

And it was here that Catholic bishops met in IIII CE to begin the work of dividing Ireland into dioceses. Division has been a part of this island's history for millennia, and a crucial chapter of it started around the corner from the cottage I have just moved into. This is the royal centre of Ireland: the coming together of the five provinces. The fifth province is *Mide*, the magical 'Otherworld', the original, mythical thin place, created in the very first century. It is also the actual centre of the island, too – the exact midway point geographically, the *Mide*, the middle of this ancient rock in the Atlantic Ocean, sea and ice sculpted, divided by a border that none of us can see.

I think of borders, of the one that has cut my island in two for the whole of my life. I think of it now with such soft tenderness. I see the moments dance in front of me – white and willowy. I am remembering joy now, and stillness. Days when we crossed over that line we have still never seen, that no one will ever really see, and how even in times of fear it still made our whole world change shape – and colour – entirely. The grey of our cold, concrete council estate was gone and in its place there was cinematic blue water all around – golden sandy beaches where the land met the sea, all held in place by hedgerows full to the brim with wild flora. Through deeply traumatic and unsettled times I have been brought or found my own way across that border to seek solace in the weeds and wilderness held in its hidden, healing, thin places. When I think of what the future may hold for all of us who have lived through the unimaginable ins and outs of the Troubles – we who can stand with one foot in the North and one in the South, we border-dwellers always weighed down by a sense of otherness – if a hard border comes back, I no longer weep as I used to at the start of this mess. We are not willing to slip back down, to lose our hoarse voices to those we cannot shout above; none of us are ready to fall into the gaps between things again. The future, the one that lies in seed deep beneath our feet, in the darkness, is ours to shape. We are ready, now; we are all of us ready for whatever the future holds; we are remembering the way through the fog.

The rain now grows softer – the swans have long passed me by and may have already landed on the lake's surface – and my thoughts have moved with them; I am thinking now of migration and of place. I am in the middle of both the land and the morning, in the halfway point of December, too, but I am looking back at things long passed by, and I am thinking of all the days that have not yet come. I am thinking about stillness and about flight. About identity and acceptance – about choices, and the way that gratitude transforms, how every cell of your body can feel like it has just been born – fresh as oak.

I think about all those I have shared a life with, and of their stories. Of who they are, on the inside and outside, on both sides of that imagined border. I think about myself, and of that shifting, liminal space between inner and outer, the belly of that soft, unseen place where we hold our rawest truths. I consider the new paths that I can already feel forming on my insides, to meet the new ones that now lie ahead of me on the outside; I can feel the shape-shifting begin. I think of the river. I see it there, as if it were right before my eyes, and I see that river properly, for the very first time.

Like that river, I am becoming an unmapped space held in this in-between place, right in this island's beating heart where borders feel like they hold no sway.

I think about the calendar year. About how the body grows

more resilient to meet the time and the place in which it finds itself. I think about journey and growth. About how the old saying about time – how it can heal – may be so much more than a truism. How time can even be a form of prayer, not to anyone or anything else. How maybe it is a form of prayer to your own self; how simply allowing yourself to *be* may be an act of deep and unimaginable healing, a way to give thanks. I think of how that story of suffering and sorrow – followed by a journey towards acceptance and hope – is a tale that is being retold in places all around our broken, beautiful world, over and over again. I think of how there are still places – parts of this earth – where light flows in like a river that has burst its banks. We hold in our open hands the strength to take suffering and turn it into song. Our voices can tell a story of hope above the cacophony of sorrow, like those wee birds that have only just left this frosty, quiet laneway, the place I feel so grateful to now call home.

The day before I left Derry I ran through St Columb's Park underneath ancient oak trees that tower above a trickling stream, the same stream I have listened to as closely as my ears have allowed since I could walk. Up the hill – mud thick underfoot, squirrels in the fallen leaves, a magpie in the lower branches of a chestnut tree, a mistle-thrush quarrelling with itself in the hidden parts above. I don't know if it was the fact that that geographical place holds so many deep memories for me, if it was the adrenaline from the cold, bright run I'd just paused from, or maybe it was just something that the air held inside it, but I felt, for the very first time, as though I was letting go.

As though each outbreath was taking something from inside me, and giving it back to the city that made me. I watched as my breath made ghostly white shapes right in front of my mouth, and I felt something inside me fall silent. There was quiet inside me – unbidden, startling – and I could hear myself, and I wanted to hear; I wanted to listen.

I was born in 1983, in the last white breath of December, at the ending of that old year. I arrived just as winter staked its claim on the north-west of Ireland, in the exact midway point of those dark, liminal, beautiful days between Christmas and New Year. I was born into a gap, in a way, a dip where the old year gathered momentum to try to make it to the crest of the hill. A wee cranny in the V of the land – I came in the lull, just before the turning of the year's circle. My birthday has always held the feeling of something not quite fully formed – a day that has not been sculpted properly, an in-between place, somehow. The date creeps up like the silence before a storm – and when it comes, it is defined by a sense of other-ness, as though the day is on the periphery of two worlds. Things nestled in the middle point of other things hold an energy all of their own. I was born into another middle, too: the middle of the Troubles. No one knew it, of course, but that year I was born cut the violent, terrifying period known as the Troubles completely in half, making a border out of time. They would continue – those tragic, terrifying years – for as many years again as they had already been raging for. There are particular periods in time – that human construct of divi-sion – that seem as though they, too, might allow for the lifting of veils, for things to happen in ways that would not (that *could not*) happen in any other moment. I think of the messages – the rich undercurrent of deep meaning – that have been revealed for me in this past year through delving deeper into the Celtic calendar, the circle of the year created by my ancestors, to help us all to get through.

There is a time for everything – for sowing, planting, harvesting. A time for holding on, and a time to let go. A time for sorrow, and a time for healing. More so, there is, simply, time. There is time for it all. We still have time to step in or out – of places, of relationships, of thought processes, of our own selves. Sometimes the snow will still be here on St Brigid's Day, and sometimes we will have a year without it coming at all. There will be years when the autumn trees seem more vibrant, more sublime, than we ever remember them being before. There will be years when we have suffered so much that we can't pick out one season from the other, never mind one day. Days when we cannot imagine ever feeling okay again, thinking that we have taken enough of it all, enough already, *enough*. Then, a change in the wind, the first bluebell, the smell of snow in the sky, the moment courses on, and everything has shape-shifted – everything is okay again, more than okay, maybe, even.

Our planet is changing vastly – so much of it is directly connected to things that are our doing, and we do not know what the future holds. What we do know, though, is that there are moments in the year, and places in the land, that hold depth of meaning far beyond the everyday. That hold weight and essence that run deeper than that which we have come so readily to take as real. The same species of moths and butter-flies that fly above the bog, a short walk across the field behind this new house, flew above people who – not that long ago in the earth's history – built vast stone circles in the hills here.

Migration, humanity, solitude, cruelty and healing. Place – our connection to the land we share – is a story we are all drawn to, in one way or another. I have been asked, over and over again, what my connection is to this place – what lines connect me to this laneway (neither blood nor marriage); what threads tie me to the middle of this island (neither biological nor historical). The only thing I know is that there is no other place I am meant to be right now; there is no other place at all. There is only the fact that when I am here it's like I can hear Ireland's heart, like I can hear my own, too. There is only the matter of all those moths and butterflies, those swallows and swans. There is only the soft, silent moon above the dark, muddy lane, and I cannot leave it. For the first time, I am ready to stay.

The longest night of the year will be here soon on this laneway, in the middle of the land. It will arrive in the very tip of the South, and in Derry, too, in the part of the North I know the best. The earth is spinning, still, on an axis that is tilted, on the same axis it has spun on since it all began.

In our Celtic landscapes, the winter solstice is an ancient seasonal rite of passage that is of deep importance and meaning. We do know not when our ancestors first stood together and paused in harmony at midwinter. Some sacred sites are aligned to the morning's rising sun. They tell us a story of the winter solstice as being important enough, over 5,000 years ago, to build a temple in its honour.

In Irish, the winter solstice is *An Grianstad*, literally translating as 'the stopping of the sun'. These days around winter solstice time are precious, the pinnacle of a darkening that calls us to rest, to be still, to heal and to hope.

The dark has been painted – over much time – as being a negative thing, a part of existence to be wary of, a bringer of fear and things best not to be thought of. Yet nature tells us a different story. The earth tells us, over and over, as each year turns the circle of itself around, that it is in the dark where beginnings are found. Life first is dreamed, birthed and shaped in the absence of light. The seeds sown in autumn germinate underground through winter before appearing as shoots in spring. Our ancestors intuitively understood this phenomenon, and held the time between Samhain and the dark-full winter solstice as the biggest gift of life: the safe place in which it all begins. In many traditions, winter solstice, the midwinter, is a time for ritual and celebrations. In a sense, this was a turning point in the battle of dark and light in the world. On the island of Ireland, our ancestors did not see winter solstice as a sad, sorrowful time, but a cusp moment in which the reverence of the equally vital energies of darkness and lightness are understood and honoured.

I think about the North, about Derry, about the changes that have arrived there, and are arriving still. I think about the crossroads that Brexit has given birth to – just at the exact moment in time that I left Derry. It is my intention to stay here, on this laneway, in the heart of Ireland, for as long as I am able. I think about the changes that – once again – I will watch from a place away from that oak-bordered city in which I was born. I think about the past, and all of the bloodshed that can never be undone. I think about the lessons that have been learned, the promises made – despite the differences between people – those promises that have long been kept. I think of the words shared between people from both sides of that once so fiercely divided city, people who had sworn never to be together in the same room as the other. I think of the light that threw itself down onto our pathways and allowed us to find the way through. I think of the laughter that found its way back, after decades of tears. I think of the brutal history we have been trying to make peace with. I think of us all, all the time these days. I think of Derry-Doire-Londonderry, that city of strong oaks, deeply rooted and full of resilience. Brexit has left scars on the city, on the whole of the UK, in fact, already, and there looks to be much worse on its way. Divisions, fear – the emphasis seems to be strictly on difference and separation, on borders and on keeping us apart, keeping us out. I have no doubt in my mind that the people of Derry – and of many parts of the North who have watched their safe spaces finally be restored in the recent past – will not stand by and watch their homes, their lives and their futures be stamped into the ground again. People who have suffered, who have been broken, who have lost too much to recollect, and have finally found a way through, will not allow the past to repeat itself so quickly. I may have just left my hometown but I am still that same wee girl who spent her childhood there, and I think I always will be. That wee girl who stood beneath a sky – ravaged by thick, black smoke – full of beautiful, winged creatures hovering and diving, dipping and soaring, glistening and calling, circling above me. I am still looking for the things that guided me through – the things that guide me through, still – and I know I always will.

•

The light is waning quickly. The moon has settled into a different part of the sky – metallic grey has been laid on top of mauve, and streaks of a much lighter grey run through it all like a collection of thin rivers; the morning is making ready for the middle part of this cold and quiet day.

It is close, so close, to the winter solstice. The year is getting itself ready to turn; the land that you are held by is holding its breath. You and that land are making ready to wait. Snow, not yet here, is on the wind, hidden in a part of the sky you cannot see. All at once, from no place at all – softly and without any sign – comes the beating of wings, powerful and other-worldly, you thought had long since left the day. The December sky above, for the most fleeting of moments, has turned to lavender; it is a world all of its own moment in time. The land that you are being held by breathes out. You breathe out, too, slowly, letting every single part of it go, watching as it all dances in the emptied sky.

You watch until you feel the loosening – the lifting – until you feel the soft, white wings leave your skin.

You watch until you see that everything else has gone; there is nothing left here.

You are completely alone under this feathery new sky; there is nothing there any more to hold you in place.

You watch as the last of the light starts to fade, as the day begins to make way for the darkness.

You sway, and you dance, remembering those curlews, and all the white moths.

Remembering those deeply rooted reeds, and the change in the wind.

Remembering them in the changed winds, dancing.

# Acknowledgements

Writing this book was a bit like the moments of an eclipse. Times came when it was too dark to see, until certain people came along, and shared their light. Wee shards of it, like ancient stone, like dust off the wing of a moth; nestling in beside my bones. There are not enough words for Thank-you, when it comes to those people. If I have left anyone out, I hope I've made it clear enough, through my actions, how grateful I am for you.

Bringers of the light:

I am grateful to Kirsty McLachlan, my agent, and one of the most amazing women I know. I don't have the words for what you mean to me. Your support and care has changed me. Thank-you for everything but mostly for the moths.

To Jo Dingley, my editor, thank-you for all that you have given me, particularly for your trust, and for such exquisite sculpting of the words.

ACKNOWLEDGEMENTS

To every single person at Canongate: Thank you. I am so proud to bring this book into the world, held safely in your strong, kind hands. Particularly to Leila Cruickshank, Vicki Rutherford, Anna Frame, Vicki Watson, Alison Rae, Gill Heeley, Francis Bickmore and Jamie Byng.

For professional support, kindness and encouragement, I am full of gratitude to Mark Avery, Laura Kenwright, Spread the Word, New Welsh Review, Martina Devlin, Jon Woolcott, Gracie and Adrian at Little Toller, Dunlin Press, Jeff, Diva and Andrew at *Caught by the River*, Wendy Barrett, Autumn and Richard at Corbel Stone Press, Clare Archibald, Sara Baume, Doireann Ní Ghríofa and many others.

Some people read this book in its early stages, in the midst of a global pandemic. I will never forget that, and I shall be ever grateful. To Seán Hewitt, Wendy Erskine, Dan Richards, Darran Anderson, Jill Crawford, Robert Macfarlane, Kathleen Jamie, Amy Liptrot and Sinéad Gleeson, with deepest gratitude. I will hold the words you gave me close to me always. To walk behind you all, on the path you carved out, moves me beyond words.

During the writing of this book I was grateful for the friend-ship of Jo Sweeting, Tanya Shadrick, Louisa Thomsen Brits, Julia O'Mahony, Jenni Doherty, Christian Donaghey, Maria Rubio, Jennie Buchanan, Kirsteen McNish, Nadia Almaini, Dan Richards and Lorna Mills for all the joy, shelter and healing love that they brought.

I am grateful to my parents for everything but most of all for keeping me safe, my brothers for teaching me to love, and my grandparents for their goodness. To the children of the man I love, I am so grateful to share a life with you. To my family, both blood, and not; this book only exists because of red threads, both visible and not, that bind me to you. It has not been easy. I love you in ancient, untamable ways. Thank-you to those who stayed.

To M, the one who lit every light in the world for me, and then taught me how.